CONTENTS

CHAPTER TWO: JESUS: A FIRST-CENTURY GALILEAN

CHAPTER THREE: JESUS THE JEW

A BELIEVER'S SEARCH FOR THE JESUS OF HISTORY

Phillip J. Cunningham, C.S.P.

PAULIST PRESS
New York/Mahwah, N.J.

The Publisher gratefully acknowledges use of the following material: Excerpts from *Death of the Messiah* by Raymond Brown. Copyright © 1994 by Associated Sulpicians of the U.S. Used by permission of Doubleday, a division of Bantam Doubleday Dell Publishing Group, Inc. Excerpts from *A Marginal Jew: Rethinking the Historical Jesus* by John P. Meier. Copyright © 1991 by John P. Meier. Used by permission of Doubleday, a division of Bantam Doubleday Dell Publishing Group, Inc.

Scripture citations, unless otherwise noted, are from the New Revised Standard Version of the Bible.

Cover design by Nighthawk Design

Library of Congress Cataloging-in-Publication Data

Cunningham, Phillip J., 1922–
   A believer's search for the Jesus of history / by Phillip J. Cunningham.
     p. cm.
   Includes bibliographical references.
   ISBN 0–8091–3814–X (alk. paper)
   1. Jesus Christ—Historicity. I. Title.
BT303.2.C86   1998
232.9′08—dc21   98-38565
                                                CIP

Published by Paulist Press
997 Macarthur Boulevard
Mahwah, New Jersey 07430

www.paulistpress.com

Printed and bound in the
United States of America

CHAPTER FOUR: JESUS AND THE BAPTIZER

CHAPTER FIVE: JESUS, THE CHARISMATIC SAGE

CHAPTER NINE: THE BEGINNING OF THE END

CHAPTER TEN: ARREST AND INTERROGATION

CHAPTER ELEVEN: THE DEATH OF JESUS

TO REVEREND RAYMOND E. BROWN, S.S.

1928–1998

FRIEND AND MENTOR

"HE LED, WE FOLLOWED."

FOREWORD

One of my earliest memories was being taken to see a passion play. I remember nothing of the performance save the climactic scene of the resurrection. Even now, sixty or more years later, I can still see it. On a totally darkened stage soldiers lie about sleeping. A bright light suddenly outlines the stone that closes the tomb. With a mighty crash the stone falls forward to reveal the risen Jesus. I had no doubt that what I saw faithfully recreated that moment in history.

As you see, like most Catholics I was raised with a rather literalistic vision of Jesus. It was a picture created by harmonizing[1] the gospel[1] accounts into a single biography. It was particularly true of the "Christmas" stories, but it characterized the presentation of the other events of Jesus' life as well. Later I would read a number of "biographies" of Christ that served to reinforce and refine my earlier view of the "Jesus of history" right through my seminary days in the 1950s and into my first years as a priest.[2]

Only later, when I took up the study of scripture again, did I learn of the nineteenth-century challenges to my rather naive views. A whole series of scholars, armed with increasingly sophisticated understandings of the language, customs and history of the first-century C.E.[3] Near East, had examined the biblical literature. Their conclusions resulted in a radical reinterpretation of that literature.

These results were gravely disturbing to many, if not most, Christians and gave rise to heated debate and controversy. The disputes continue. Unfortunately, the Catholic Church's reaction at the time was to condemn such conclusions and to forbid their being taught. Hence, I was able to pass through the seminary and early years as a priest with my childhood vision of Jesus virtually intact.

1

As the *New Jerome Biblical Commentary*[4] observes: "The first 40 years of the 20th century...were dark days for Catholic biblical scholarship."[5] The tide turned when, in 1943, Pius XII issued the encyclical *Divino Afflante Spiritu.* Seven years later the same pontiff promulgated *Humani Generis.* Though these documents by no means approved all the conclusions of the earlier scripture studies, they did open the way for Catholic scholars to use more freely the results of that scientific research.

After the Second Vatican Council and the opportunity to study with such men as Raymond Brown and Joseph Fitzmyer the full impact of the new scholarship began to influence my own understanding of the Old and New Testaments.[6] Frankly, I probably was too quick to embrace the more radical interpretations that were proposed. In abandoning a rather literalistic vision of the gospel story I may have "thrown the baby out with the bath water." I became increasingly skeptical that there was any possibility of recovering more than the barest biographical material about Jesus. As we will see, mine was a view shared by many of the leading scripture scholars, even to this day.

My attention increasingly focused on the communities of believers that lay behind the documents of both the Hebrew Bible and the New Testament. History and the related archeological disciplines enable us to place scripture into a concrete setting. This helps us to understand the beliefs of these peoples as well as the historical circumstances that shaped many of those beliefs. What I learned can be seen in my *Exploring Scripture: How the Bible Came to Be.*

Later, in writing *Mark: The Good News Preached to the Romans,* I focused on one such community, a group of Christians living in late-first-century Rome. The first of the gospels is seen not so much as a biography of Jesus as it is a "biography" of an early church.[7] In doing this I was particularly indebted to two short works by Raymond Brown, *The Churches the Apostles Left Behind* and *The Community of the Beloved Disciple.* In them and elsewhere Father Brown has shown how early Christian communities shaped the gospels as well as the other documents making up the New Testament.

Here is the challenge. As the various historical sciences have given us an ever deeper understanding of the Hebrew Bible and the earliest Christian literature, that vivid but literalistic picture of Jesus has begun to fade. It is understandable why believers, becoming aware of this, have rejected such conclusions, preferring to cling to their traditional views. Their choice seems all the wiser when it is known that scripture scholars themselves bitterly dispute some of these conclusions.

But even if it is granted that one cannot recreate a Jesus of history with the clarity of the literalistic vision, is there nothing of that Jesus available to us? Are the investigations of modern scripture scholarship of no use to the believer? More seriously, are the results of such studies necessarily a threat to the faith of the believer? I am convinced that none of these possibilities need be true. I hope to show in the chapters to come that, on the contrary, the search for the Jesus of history will enrich our faith.

The literature in the field is vast, wide-ranging and even contradictory. In carrying out such a search, I will make my most frequent references to the works of four contemporary scripture scholars. These are John P. Meier's *A Marginal Jew: Rethinking The Historical Jesus,*[8] John Dominic Crossan's *The Historical Jesus: The Life of a Mediterranean Jewish Peasant,*[9] Raymond E. Brown's *The Death of the Messiah*[10] and Geza Vermes's *Jesus the Jew* and *The Religion of Jesus the Jew.*

What follows, of course, is not so much *my* search but *our* search as believers. Such being true, there are certain implications. Ours is a faith seeking understanding, not simply seeking proof. We are not disinterested observers. For us, Jesus of Nazareth is, as Paul told the Romans, "[God's] Son, who was descended from David according to the flesh and was declared to be Son of God with power according to the spirit of holiness by resurrection from the dead" (Rom 1:3–4). Nothing to follow should be understood as contradicting our belief in either the Divinity or the humanity of Jesus.

Journeys of discovery, by definition, lead one down new trails and the new is often challenging, even frightening when first encountered. The temptation is to turn back, to return to the familiar. Usually, however, what is new is enriching; it broadens as well as deepens our understanding. It is my hope that our search will have just that rewarding effect. Please join me now as we begin our search for the Jesus of history.

EVENTS SURROUNDING THE JESUS OF HISTORY

Before The Common Era

63	Pompey Conquers Jerusalem
44	Caesar assassinated
40	Herod (the Great) appointed the King of Judea
30	Octavian (Augustus) becomes emperor of the Roman Empire
6	Judea annexed by Rome
c.4	Jesus of Nazareth born
4	The death of Herod

Common Era

6	Judea becomes a Roman province
c.10	Saul of Tarsus (Paul) born
14	Tiberius becomes emperor
c.28	Jesus of Nazareth begins his public life
c.30	Jesus is executed at the orders of Pontius Pilate
c.36	Martyrdom of Stephen
	Conversion of Paul
37	Caligula becomes emperor
	Herod Agrippa I appointed ruler of Judea and surrounding areas.
c.40	Persecution of Christians under Herod Agrippa
42	Claudius becomes emperor
44	Palestine returns to direct Roman rule
46	Paul begins the first of his missionary journeys
48	Jews expelled from Rome
c.50	The First Letter to the Thessalonians, Paul's earliest writing
54	Nero becomes emperor
c.58	Letter to the Romans, possibly Paul's final letter
60	Paul journeys to Rome
64	Persecution of Christians in Rome under Nero
66	The First Jewish Revolt
c.67	Death of Paul
69	Vespasian becomes emperor
70	Judea conquered and Jerusalem destroyed under Titus
c.75	The Gospel of Mark
c.77	*History of the Jewish War,* Flavius Josephus
79	Titus becomes emperor
81	Domitian becomes emperor
c.85	The Gospel of Matthew
	The Gospel of Luke
c.94	*Jewish Antiquities,* Flavius Josephus
95	Persecution of Christians under Domitian
c.100	The Gospel of John
c.110	*Annals,* Cornelius Tacitus
c.112	*Epistles,* Pliny the Younger
c.121	*Lives of the Caesars,* Gaius Suetonius
132	The Second Jewish Revolt

•Besides the letters listed here, those to the Galatians, Philippians, two to the Corinthians and to Philemon are considered authentic.

INTRODUCTION

I. THE "REAL" JESUS

In the search for any historical figure the biographer examines the sources, the records of both the person and of the time and place in which he or she lived. Yet such sources, no matter how complete, never give us complete access to the "real" person. Ultimately that reality always escapes us. Take the example of the late president, Richard Nixon. No public figure has left a more detailed body of evidence surrounding both his public and private lives. Nevertheless, just who was the "real" Richard Nixon is a matter of continuing debate among scholars. Another example would be Abraham Lincoln. He is one of the most closely studied figures in American history; yet each generation seems to produce new insights into this enigmatic figure.[1]

The above are relatively recent examples. The challenge to the historian becomes only more monumental as we move back through time. The sources soon become sketchy or nonexistent. Increasingly one must rely on records that were not composed under the standards for history we have today. Our knowledge of some of the most outstanding figures in the past, such as Alexander the Great or Socrates, rests upon the thinnest of resources. So, as you see, a historian's search for the "real" can be a frustrating task.

In the light of this we can see the reason for an important distinction made by Meier at the beginning of his first chapter: "The historical Jesus is not the real Jesus. The real Jesus is not the historical Jesus."[2] In Palestine,[3] almost two millennia ago, there lived, worked and died a "real" Jesus of Nazareth, just as there was a "real" George Washington in Virginia two centuries ago. In our search for the Jesus of history we will strive to learn all we can about the "real" Jesus, but that Jesus will always escape us; the reality will always be more, much more, than we can discover.

II. THE JESUS OF FAITH

The tools for the scientific study of history have been available for only little more than a century. Some of the most effective instruments used in such investigations are of even more recent discovery. We might say that our search for the Jesus of history has only been made possible in modern times. However, as Meier stresses: "More than a millennium and half of Christians believed firmly in Jesus Christ without having any clear idea of or access to the historical Jesus as understood today."[4] Of course, the same situation persists for many Christians today.

What then is the relationship between the Jesus as the object of our faith and the Jesus for whom we are searching? Meier points out that "the Jesus of history is not and cannot be the object of Christian faith."[5] Luke Timothy Johnson is explicit: "I will argue that Christian faith has never—either at the start or now—been *based on historical reconstructions of Jesus,* even though Christian faith has always involved some historical claims concerning Jesus."[6] Of course, the foundation of our faith must lie in reality, in the words and deeds of the "real" Jesus. This is the Jesus Paul of Tarsus had in mind when he spoke of "the gospel concerning [God's] Son, who was descended from David according to the flesh and was declared to be Son of God with power according to the spirit of holiness by resurrection from the dead, Jesus Christ our Lord" (Rom 1:3–4).

Moreover, as we read in the Letter to the Hebrews: "Jesus Christ is the same yesterday and today and forever" (Heb 13:8). The "real" Jesus, the foundation of our faith, remains unchanged, but we change. Our understanding of Jesus has constantly altered as Christianity moved through the centuries.[7] In searching for the Jesus of history we see the same process. We continue to learn more about him as the various archeological and related sciences perfect their methods. Also, as time passes, our own perspective is transformed. We always stand in a new place as we look back through time.

III. THE JESUS OF HISTORY

A. The Faded Fresco

In our search we will make use of the same methodology employed to recover any historic figure. Here, however, we face the restrictions imposed by the limited record we have at our disposal. As Meier puts it: "Of its very nature, this quest can reconstruct only fragments of a mosaic, the faint outline of a faded fresco that allows of many interpretations....The historical Jesus may give us fragments of the 'real' person, but nothing more."[8] Ours must be a modest expectation.

With expectations of unearthing only the "fragments of a mosaic, the faint outline of a faded fresco," one wonders why anyone engages in the search. Yet, it obviously has not discouraged Meier himself as he launches a three-volume study subtitled *Rethinking the Historical Jesus*. Given the amount of contemporary literature on the same subject, it would seem that few are inhibited in their search by such small hopes. Still we might ask why we should engage in the quest.

B. Motivations for the Search

In a chapter entitled "Why Bother?" Meier gives his reasons for pursuing a study of the historical Jesus in the face of limited results. Such a study, he stresses, opposes "any attempt to reduce faith in Christ to a content-less cipher, a mythic symbol, or a timeless archetype....The Christian faith is an affirmation of and adherence to a particular person who said and did particular things in a particular time and place in human history."[9] Pursuing the historical Jesus prevents the real Jesus from fading into a "philosophy of life" or similarly vague "movement." The Jesus of history provides the Jesus of faith with a solid anchor in reality.

Also the quest for the Jesus of history prevents "any attempt by pious Christians...to swallow up the real humanity of Jesus into an 'orthodox' emphasis on his divinity."[10] It is a danger more common than one might realize. In large part the outcry occasioned by Martin Scorsese's film *The Last Temptation of Christ* stemmed from those who were scandalized by the depiction of a too-human Jesus. Similarly, the frequent artistic presentation of Christ as an idealized figure reflects an overly divinized Jesus.[11] The real Jesus, emerging however faintly from the historical Jesus, keeps us in touch with his fundamental humanity; as Meier puts it, "a person as truly and fully human—with all the galling limitations that involves—as any other human being."[12]

Unfortunately, over the centuries, there has been the tendency, as Meier puts it, "to 'domesticate' Jesus for a comfortable, respectable, bourgeois Christianity."[13] It is understandable for those living in a society ostensibly Christian to see Jesus as conformist rather than radical. However, the Jesus revealed by our study of history was obviously at odds with the society and culture in which he lived. In fact, it is most likely that his refusal to be "domesticated" led directly to his execution.

On the other hand, as Meier cautions, "the historical Jesus is not easily co-opted for programs of political revolution either....The historical Jesus subverts not just some ideologies but all ideologies, including liberation theology."[14] Here we touch on a very sensitive issue. The followers of Jesus must certainly oppose oppression in all its forms, social, political and economic. There is, to use current terminology, a *preferential option* for the poor. Yet the Jesus of history prevents us from absorbing Jesus into any contemporary revolutionary guise.

To Meier's reasons I add my own. True, what we find at the end of our search may be "only fragments of a mosaic, the faint outline of a faded fresco." Yet, behind the fresco, faded though it may be, is *someone*. Within the limited record of Jesus' deeds and words that has come down to us there is a real person to be found. Our awareness of that reality gives to those deeds and words a meaning that disembodied traditions would not have.

Our search for the Jesus of history, no matter how modest our hopes, can serve to give our faith a firmer anchor in reality. The object of our faith is not the Jesus of history, but our search for that Jesus keeps us mindful of the "real" Jesus, the "real" person who lies behind "the good news of Jesus Christ, the Son of God" (Mk 1:1).

Chapter One

THE SOURCES

I. THE NON-CHRISTIAN SOURCES

A. *Josephus*

Jesus himself left no writings, nor are there contemporary records of his existence. Thus we begin our search with references to Jesus found in early historians. Unfortunately, though he is certainly the most widely known figure in human history, there are only a few allusions to Jesus in the works from the first century of the common era. Among those of particular significance are the ones found in works by Flavius Josephus.

Born Joseph ben Matthias in 37 C.E., Josephus led the Jewish forces in Galilee at the beginning of the revolt against Rome in 66 C.E. Josephus was captured, but with the patronage of Vespasian, the Roman commander and later emperor, he became a citizen of Rome. Josephus wrote two major historical works, *The Jewish War* (75–79 C.E.) and *Jewish Antiquities* (93–94 C.E.). Both are highly regarded resources on life in Palestine under Roman domination. Josephus died at the end of the first century.

In a passage found in his *Jewish Antiquities* Josephus mentions a James, whom he describes as "the brother of Jesus who is called the Messiah."[1] We know of such a James from St. Paul, who refers to "James the Lord's brother" in his letter to the Galatians (1:19). Later in the same document we find a reference to "James and Cephas and John, who were acknowledged pillars [of the Jerusalem Christian community]" (2:9). Apparently there were several men named James, and Josephus uses the reference to Jesus in order to identify the James of whom he is speaking. This indicates that by the latter part of the first

century a "Jesus who is called the Messiah" was well-known to Josephus's readers.

There is also in the *Jewish Antiquities* a direct reference to Jesus
himself. Unfortunately, the version that has come down to us shows
evidence of later Christian-inspired additions. Though the matter is
debated, most scholars regard the following as coming from the hand of
Josephus:

> At that time there appeared Jesus, a wise man....For he was a doer of
> startling deeds, a teacher of people who receive the truth with pleasure.
> And he gained a following both among many Jews and among many of
> Greek origin....And when Pilate, because of an accusation made by
> leading men among us, condemned him to the cross, those who had
> loved him previously did not cease to do so....And up until this very day
> the tribe of Christians (named after him) has not died out."[2]

Josephus thus affirms that early in the first century C.E. one named
Jesus appeared in Palestine. He was "a wise man...a doer of startling
deeds, a teacher." He gathered a following, but upon an unspecified
accusation made by the Jewish leadership, he was executed at the order
of Pontius Pilate. As Pilate was the Roman representative in Palestine
from 26 to 36 C.E., Jesus would have perished within that period. Further, Josephus records that followers of Jesus, known as Christians, still
exist as the century ends. Thus Josephus firmly anchors Jesus in the
history of the period.

B. *Tacitus and Others*

At the beginning of the second century the Roman historian, Tacitus
(ca. 56–ca. 118) relates in his *Annals* the events surrounding a great fire
that destroyed much of Rome during the reign of Emperor Nero:

> To suppress this rumor [that he had started the fire], Nero fabricated
> scapegoats—and punished with every refinement the notoriously
> depraved Christians (as they were popularly called). Their originator,
> Christ, had been executed in Tiberias's reign by the governor of Judaea,
> Pontius Pilate. But in spite of this temporary setback the deadly supersti-
> tion had broken out afresh, not only in Judaea (where the mischief had
> started) but even in Rome. All degraded and shameful practices collect
> and flourish in the capital.[3]

Tiberius reigned as emperor between 14 and 37 C.E., again indicating, as did Josephus, that Jesus lived and died in Palestine early in the first century.

Another Roman historian, Suetonius (ca. 70–after 122), has the following reference in his *The Twelve Caesars* to an incident in the life of the Emperor Claudius: "Because the Jews at Rome caused continuous disturbances at the instigation of Chrestus, he expelled them from the city."[4] *Chrestus* is the Latin for "Christ." The expulsion occurred in 48 C.E. The citation indicates the existence of Jesus prior to that date. There are similar references to Christians, and thus to the prior existence of Jesus, by Pliny the Younger and Lucian of Samosata, both in the second century C.E. Beyond these there is no mention, direct or indirect, of Jesus in the non-Christian historians active in the first two centuries.

II. THE CHRISTIAN SOURCES

A. Developing the Traditions

1. THE EARLY YEARS

The authentic[5] letters of St. Paul, written between 50 and 58 C.E., are the earliest Christian documents we have. Later in the first century Christian material becomes more common. It must be kept in mind that the ability to read at the time was not widespread. Moreover, manuscripts were rare and expensive. On the other hand, people were able to commit remarkable amounts of lore to memory. Thus, for over a generation what we know of Jesus' deeds and words was passed down in the oral tradition of his followers. Those who had seen and heard Jesus during his public life in Galilee and Judea told of their experiences to those who were later drawn to his message. Early on, these followers of Jesus were being called Christians.[6]

In estimating the growth of Christianity, Rodney Stark[7] put the number of Christians at one thousand in 40 C.E., fourteen hundred in 50 C.E. and seventy-five hundred by the end of the first century. At first the Christians were Jewish or converts to Judaism. In a short time the message of Jesus began to reach the Gentiles. We now enter a period of transition. What had originated in a Jewish environment now entered the Hellenistic culture of the empire. Now we see conflicts developing between the Hellenized and non-Hellenized Christians described in Paul's letters and in the Book of Acts.

There was another transition. Those who first saw and heard Jesus were the inhabitants of rural villages in lower Galilee. With the passage of time most Christians lived in urban areas. As Wayne A. Meeks observes: "It was in the cities of the Roman Empire that Christianity, though born in the village culture of Palestine, had its greatest successes until well after the time of Constantine."[8] A message first hear by Galilean villagers had to be made meaningful to the city-dwellers of the empire.

2. THE COMING OF THE CHURCH

At first, as noted, the followers of Jesus were part of Judaism. They apparently attended the synagogues while at the same time seeking to convince others to accept their beliefs about Jesus. Hence, the conflict reported by Suetonius. The breach gradually widened. By the final years of the first century most Christians were no longer part of the Jewish religion.

Sadly, that parting was not a happy one, and it brought with it a further challenge for the Christians. Rome was generally tolerant of local religions and the various religious sects *provided* there was participation in the state (imperial) religion. From experience Rome knew that Jews could not be forced to comply with such a rule. As a result, they we given exemptions to the law. Christians lost such immunity when they were no longer seen as a Jewish sect.

Thus, unable to reveal their religion publicly, Christians met privately in members' homes. "Our sources give us good reason to be think the [individual household] was the basic unit in the establishment of Christianity in the city, as it was, indeed, the basic unit of the city itself."[9] These became known as "house churches."[10] The larger cities certainly had more than one house church, and at first they were more or less independent of each other. It was not long, however, before such small communities would meet together to form a "local church."

As Reverend Larry Boadt, C.S.P., author of *Reading the Old Testament,* notes:

> On one level this (the formation of the local church) is reasonable enough. But Paul's and the other letters are addressed to local churches that were

founded by the apostles and evangelists, not house by house, but from the start by preaching to the whole community (private correspondence). In whatever manner the local churches formed, it is with their appearance that we find individuals being referred to as *episcopoi,* the Greek for "overseer,"[11] and exercising authority over the Christian communities.

During this early period traditions about the words and deeds of Jesus were being passed on as part of religious celebrations, perhaps during early forms of the eucharistic services. In Luke's account of the two disciples' encounter with Jesus on the way to Emmaus we have a specific reference to such a service: "When [Jesus] was at the table with them, he took bread, blessed and broke it, and gave it to them" (Lk 24:30; see also 1 Cor 11:23–26). It is preceded by Jesus himself giving what may have been the customary "sermon" at such a gathering: "Then beginning with Moses and all the prophets, he interpreted to them the things about himself in all the scriptures" (Lk 24:27).

Around the middle of the century these oral traditions were written down and then circulated to other Christian communities as followers of Jesus moved about the empire. Sadly, from our point of view, these earliest documents disappeared or were incorporated into later manuscripts. As we come to the latter part of the first century, more and more such material came into existence and, happily for us, more and more of it survived.

B. *The Coming of the Canon*

With increasing contact between the Christian communities a process began that had a profound effect on the written traditions about Jesus. As the early manuscripts[12] were circulated from church to church, collections of such documents began to appear and these also were circulated. Christians had already accepted the Jewish scriptures as authoritative. Now writings from Christian sources began to receive similar recognition.

At first there was some disagreement among the churches as to which writings should be so regarded, but gradually uniformity prevailed. Raymond Brown observes: "By 200, then, the Gospels, the Pauline epistles, Acts, I Peter, and I John had come into general acceptance. By the end of the 4th cent. in the [Latin] and [Greek] churches there was general acceptance of the 27-book canon[13] of the [New Testament]."[14]

Not all the early Christian writings were included in the canon. Why some and not others? Raymond Brown cites three reasons:

> (1) Apostolic origin, real or putative,[15] was very important....(2) Most of the [New Testament] works were addressed to particular Christian communities, and the history and importance of the community involved had much to do with the preservation and even the ultimate acceptance of these works....(3) Conformity with the rule of faith was a criterion of acceptance.[16]

It is even possible, Brown concludes, that chance played a role in the survival of some documents rather than others.

C. The Canonical Gospels

1. INTRODUCTION

As our search is for the Jesus of history, those Christians documents known as the four gospels (from the Old English meaning "good word") will be of primary interest. The balance of the New Testament affirms that Jesus of Nazareth existed but says little if anything about his life. St. Paul, the earliest witness we have among the Christian authors, is typical. Apparently he did not arrive in Palestine until after the death of Jesus and tells his readers almost nothing of the Nazorean's deeds or words. His letters, as with the New Testament writings other than the gospels, tell us far more about the history of the Christian Church than about the Jesus of history.

We shall follow the custom of referring to the gospels under their traditional titles: Mark, Matthew, Luke and John. However, it is the opinion of current scripture studies that the actual authorships are unknown. Raymond Brown expresses the general opinion: "In fact, there is no longer an official Roman Catholic position about the identity of the writer of any biblical book."[17] Attribution to figures referred to in the New Testament was made in the second century C.E.

2. THE SYNOPTICS

Between the mid-60s and the 90s of the common era the gospels of Mark, Matthew and Luke make their appearance. Because they exhibit roughly the same chronology (or synopsis) for events in Jesus' life, they are called the synoptic gospels. Most scholars attribute the resemblance to the fact that the authors of Matthew and Luke used Mark as a guide in composing their gospels. Mark would thus have been written first.[18]

Besides their dependence on Mark, Matthew and Luke each incorporate unique material reflecting the traditions and concerns of their individual communities.[19] In addition, Matthew and Luke also share a common tradition, not found in Mark. It is customary for scholars to refer to this material as *Q* from the German word for "source," *Quelle.* As a source, *Q* is largely composed of sayings attributed to Jesus and is the subject of much debate.[20] Was it ever a separate document? If so we have no record of it as such. Does it represent the beliefs of an early group of Christians? Burton L. Mack in *The Lost Gospel* develops such a view in great detail. Later we will return to a discussion of *Q.*

3. JOHN

On reading the Fourth Gospel, it becomes immediately obvious that John represents a further stage in the formation of the gospel message. The gospel appeared late in the first or very early in the second century. It was a time when new challenges were facing the Christian communities. The gospel of John and the three letters associated with it reveal a response to these challenges.[21] However, scholars believe that John does preserve some very early traditions about Jesus.

D. The Other Gospels

1. IN GENERAL

The gospel as a literary form was an innovation of Mark. It was apparently he who first wrote down the "good news" in narrative form. His opus not only influenced Matthew, Luke and John but also numerous other writers of the first and second centuries as well. These writings were not accepted in the New Testament canon and thus have suffered much over the passage of time. In *The Other Gospels,* edited by Ron Cameron, we have the texts or partial texts of sixteen such documents. Unfortunately for our purposes, while these "gospels" may say much about early Christianity, they add little to what we know of Jesus himself.

2. THE GOSPEL OF THOMAS

One of these other gospels is of interest to us, however. In 1945, near the Egyptian city of Nag Hammadi, a number of Coptic[22] manuscripts were discovered. Among them was a document known as the gospel of Thomas. Marvin Meyer, in *The Gospel of Thomas: The Hidden Sayings of Jesus,* notes that "the Gospel of Thomas must have been composed during the second century or even the latter part of the first century."[23] The more conservative dating would be to the beginning of the third century.[24]

The document is a collection of sayings attributed to Jesus, a hundred and fourteen in number. Ninety of these are parallels or variants of texts found in the synoptic gospels. The remainder are unique to *Thomas.* It is possible that some of these quotations are actually earlier forms of traditions going back to Jesus himself.[25] In its form *The Gospel of Thomas* resembles *Q* to some degree. In our search for the Jesus of history, *Thomas* will be of marginal help.

III. THE NATURE OF HISTORY

A. *The Criteria*

What makes all of these sources problematic in our search for the Jesus of history is that their purposes were not precisely biographical. The noncanonical material sought to augment earlier sources and to shape those sources to support variant understandings of the Christian message. Those documents that would form the New Testament sought to preserve the traditions of Christian communities as well, but they also sought to shape those traditions to meet the needs and concerns of those communities. Thus even in the canonical gospels it is not easy to recover the earlier version of those traditions.

Scholars, in their attempts at such a recovery, generally employ several criteria. For instance, one is "that the early Church would hardly have gone out of its way to create material that only embarrassed its creator or weakened its position in arguments with opponents."[26] Any material that does so would likely reflect an early stage of the tradition. A prime example, as we shall see, is Jesus' baptism by John. It creates an awkward situation that the evangelists must explain or, as in the case of John's gospel, simply ignore.

Another criterion is that of dissimilarity. Norman Perrin describes it as follows:

> The teaching of Jesus was set in the context of ancient Judaism, and in many respects that teaching must have been variations on themes from the religious life of ancient Judaism. But if we are to seek that which is most characteristic of Jesus, it will be found not in the things which he shares with his contemporaries, but in the things where in he differs from them.[27]

Meier cites Jesus' prohibition of oaths (Mt 5:34–37) as an example of such a dissimilarity.[28]

As noted, we do have sources that are independent of one another, such as Mark, *Q,* Paul and John. Words and deeds of Jesus found in two or more of these sources have an increased probability of being from an early tradition. One can also assume that the message of Jesus reflects a certain level of consistency. Having established a theme as being an early aspect of Jesus' preaching, we do not expect him to have said something contradictory later. Similarly, a text reflecting the theme would have an increased possibility of authenticity.

Finally, we should keep in mind what we do know historically about Jesus. He was executed at the behest of some Jewish officials and the Roman procurator. We would expect to discover in the authentic traditions about Jesus of Nazareth what brought about such a fate. As Meier puts it: "A Jesus whose words and deeds would not alienate people, especially powerful people, is not the historical Jesus."[29] As we proceed we will be referring to these criteria in our effort to recover that historical Jesus.

B. The Challenge

In *Who Killed Jesus?* John Dominic Crossan distinguishes "history remembered" from "prophecy historicized."[30] The former is history in the usual sense. In the latter, however, material from the Hebrew scriptures is used to create what appears to be history but is actually not. At times it will be obvious that such creativity is being exercised. In other instances it will not be so clear-cut. In commenting on the conclusions of Raymond Brown, Crossan observed, "Ray Brown is 80 percent in the direction of history remembered. I'm 80 percent in the opposite direction."[31] Later, when we come to the final days of Jesus' life, the distinction becomes particularly crucial.

Our challenge now is to use imagination, conjecture and educated guesses to delineate from that "faint outline of a faded fresco" what we can learn of the Jesus of history, the Jesus who is also the object of our faith.

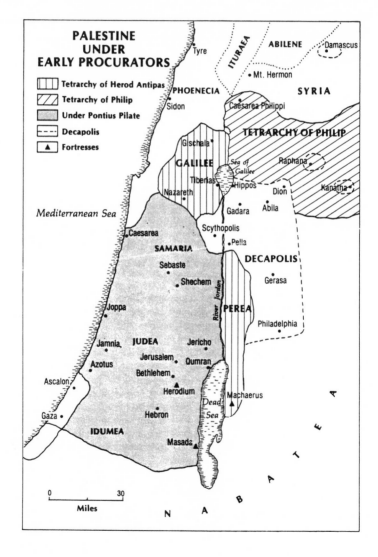

Chapter Two

JESUS: A FIRST-CENTURY GALILEAN

I. WHEN JESUS LIVED

Crucial to any biography is knowing when the subject was born and when he died. These dates enable to the writer to place his study in the broader context of history. In ancient times, before accurate records were routine, such dates can be difficult to determine, and such is the case with Jesus. Matthew and Luke, while they disagree on some points concerning Jesus' early life, both state that Jesus was born during the reign of Herod the Great (Mt 2:1, Lk 1:5), that is, prior to 4 B.C.E.[1] But, how many years prior? Luke remarks that "Jesus was about thirty years old when he began his work" (3:23). That would place the date on which Jesus was born as just a few years before the death of Herod.

As we saw in the previous chapter, early sources agree that Jesus died while Pontius Pilate was procurator of Judea. There would be general agreement that, "thanks to Josephus, with supplementary information supplied by Philo, Tacitus, Suetonius, Cassio Dio, and Eusebius, we can calculate that Pilate held his office from A.D. 26 to 36 (or very early 37)."[2] Similarly, "we emerge with a range between 30 and 33 for the death of Jesus."[3] Jesus would have been between thirty-five and forty years of age when he died, actually about the normal life-span for the period.

19

II. WHERE JESUS LIVED

A. *Galilee*

1. GEOGRAPHY AND HISTORY

Where someone grew up and among what sort of people that person lived are equally crucial to the biographer. The political, social and cultural milieu of a person's life is bound to have extensive influence. Mark says simply, "In those days Jesus came from Nazareth of Galilee" (1:9). The gospel record is unanimous in associating Jesus with the area known as Galilee. Matthew and Luke identify Jesus as a Galilean, as does John (Mt 26:69; Lk 22:59; 23:5–6; Jn 7:41). More precisely, we can locate the life and ministry of Jesus with an area known as Lower Galilee.

Lower Galilee of the first century was an area stretching from the coastal plain on the west to the Sea of Galilee on the east, some thirty-five miles at its widest. From the foothills of the mountains in northern Galilee, the territory reached south to the Valley of the Jezreel, about the same distance. It was basically farm country. Its small towns and villages lay in the midst of fields, groves and pastures. There were only two cities of any size, Sepphoris and Tiberias. These apparently vied with each other for the role of capital city of the area.

Galilee itself was part of the territory occupied by the Israelites when they entered the land of Canaan in the thirteenth century B.C.E. Five centuries later the territory was conquered by the Assyrians, the so-called Ten Tribes[4] were deported and other peoples entered the land. Isaiah speaks of it as the "Galilee[5] of the nations [Gentiles]" (9:1). Nevertheless, a Jewish minority apparently remained. It was not until after the annexation of Galilee to the Maccabean-Hasmonean kingdom (ca. 100 B.C.E.) that the territory again became substantially Jewish.

The independent Jewish kingdom fell to the Roman forces under Pompey in 63 B.C.E. and became part of the province of Syria. Unlike Judea to the south, Galilee was not later subject to direct rule by representatives of Rome. It enjoyed a degree of independence, being ruled by the Herodian Tetrarch Antipas (4 B.C.E.–40 C.E.). The Roman rule that Jesus experienced during his life in Galilee was not as oppressive a presence as it must have been for the Judeans. The tax collectors Jesus knew, odious as they were, were at least Galileans.

2. SOCIOLOGY

Dr. Geza Vermes notes: "The Galilee of Jesus was populous and relatively wealthy."[6] The difficulty was in the distribution of that wealth, a distribution similar to that of many third-world countries today. Only a small, even microscopic, percentage of the population could be called wealthy. A few more—merchants, craftsmen, farmers with larger amounts of land—had some degree of security. "Small farmers in particular led a precarious existence, sometimes at the subsistence level, subject as they were to the vagaries of weather, market prices, inflation, grasping rulers, wars and heavy taxes (both civil and religious)."[7] Yet these were not the worst off. Below them were the "day laborers, hired servants, traveling craftsmen, and dispossessed farmers forced into banditry."[8] At the bottom of the heap were the slaves who worked the great estates, though this group does not seem to have been common in Galilee.

3. REVOLUTIONARY REPUTATION

The overall impression one gets from reading the gospels is one of Jesus moving through a landscape at peace. It is true that the Galilean reign of Herod Antipas (4 B.C.E.–40 C.E.) was an brief era of quiescence in an otherwise turbulent period. "It was, among other things, this relatively peaceful state of society that enabled Jesus to undertake a multi-year itinerant mission around Galilee and beyond."[9] A generation or so later, with the onset of the Jewish War, such a ministry would have been impossible.

Yet Vermes can still observe: "From the middle of the last pre-Christian century [Galilee] was the most troublesome of all Jewish districts."[10] Behind a facade of peace violence was brewing. The politico-religious party known as Zealots had its origins in lower Galilee with the revolutionary, Judas the Galilean.[11] Descendants of Judas were active in the tragic events leading to the open warfare between the Jews and the imperial forces beginning in 66 C.E. Vermes writes: "The struggle against the Empire was nevertheless not just a family business, but a full-scale Galilean activity in the first century A.D."[12] In fact, "it is not surprising that to the first-century A.D. Palestinian establishment the word 'Galilean' ceased merely to refer to a particular geographical area and took on a dark political connotation of a possible association with Judas the Galilean."[13]

Whatever were the peaceful conditions that Galilee enjoyed at the time of Jesus there must have been ramifications of these revolutionary struggles that touched his life. The precarious conditions of rural life, as noted above, fueled the unrest. A bad harvest, an increase in taxes, these would have immediately threatened the well-being of Jesus and his family as it did that of his neighbors. The aspirations for change that swirled through Galilee surely must have affected Jesus. Yet, "strange though it may seem, Jesus grew up and conducted much of his ministry in an uncommonly peaceful oasis sheltered from the desert whirlwind that was most of Palestinian history."[14] That quiescent hiatus was certainly essential to Jesus' ministry as we know it.

B. Nazareth

"Jesus was not an urbanite. The cities of Galilee—Sepphoris, Tiberias—do not figure in the accounts of his life."[15] The gospels identify Jesus with the village of Nazareth. In Mark we have, "In those days Jesus came from Nazareth of Galilee" (1:9). Matthew and Luke, though citing different explanations,[16] also account for Jesus presence in that Galilean village. In John, when Philip speaks of "Jesus son of Joseph from Nazareth," Nathanael replies scornfully, "Can anything good come out of Nazareth?" (1:45–46). It was here that Jesus spent all but the last few years of his life in obscurity.

Archeological discoveries indicate the site was occupied as early as two thousand years before the common era. However, it probably became the village Jesus knew only some two centuries earlier.[17] In his day it was a few simple dwellings clustered around a village square in the midst of small fields and pastures. Excavations indicate the houses were simple, one-room structures, usually backed up to a cave cut into the hillside. The family and its animals shared the same living area. The village itself, with possibly two thousand inhabitants,[18] is unmentioned in ancient sources outside the New Testament.

III. THE HIDDEN YEARS

A. Infancy

The Jewish and Gentile sources make no mention of Jesus' early years. Paul, the earliest Christian source, has minimal information about Jesus' public ministry and nothing of events prior to that. Mark, the first of the gospels, begins his account with the encounter between John the Baptizer and Jesus. It is only in the latter part of the first century that we find what purport to be accounts of Jesus' first years. These opening chapters of Matthew and Luke are customarily referred to as the infancy narratives, though they cover a longer period of his life.

In evaluating these chapters as history we have to keep in mind the observation of Raymond Brown in his monumental study *The Birth of the Messiah:* "We have no real knowledge that any or all of the infancy material came from a tradition for which there was a corroborating witness."[19] Without such corroboration we must proceed with caution when using the infancy narratives in our search for the Jesus of history.

In fact, the infancy narratives make such extensive references to passages from the Jewish scriptures that I'm afraid the picture they give the reader is far more "prophecy historicized" than "history remembered." Moreover, the accounts in Matthew and Luke of Jesus' birth and early years are contradictory on some points (see note 16). Yet, as we are reminded: "Whether or not the infancy narratives are history, whether or not they are based on eye-witness testimony, whether or not they had a pre-Gospel existence, Matthew and Luke thought they were appropriate introductions to the career and significance of Jesus."[20] As such, however, they are not of much help in our search for the Jesus of history.

B. The Woodworker

Though direct evidence about Jesus' life before his public ministry is scarce, we are not without clues. With these we can recapture the outline ("faded fresco") of that life. For instance, in the gospel record we have the following: "Is not this the carpenter?" (Mk 6:3) and "Is not this the carpenter's son?" (Mt 13:55). As it was common for a father to pass on his trade to his son, it is possible to take both of these statements at face value, concluding that Jesus was a carpenter by trade.

It is an occupation that usually brings to our minds the construction of housing, but in a deforested area like ancient Palestine, such a liberal use of wood was not possible. In our milieu, the trade would have been closer to a woodworker, someone who fashioned tables, chairs, beds, even farm implements such as plows, rakes and flails.[21]

As a woodworker Jesus would have put in a hard day's labor, but at the same time, as a craftsman, he probably enjoyed a modest level of security. There is no reason to believe that he or his family lived in the crushing poverty that burdened so many of his contemporaries. One can suspect Jesus and his family—along with other craftsmen, local merchants and farmers with the larger fields—were among the better-off citizens of Nazareth.

C. Was Jesus Literate?

This is not a trivial question; a literate Jesus makes more understandable a mature figure who appears well-versed in Jewish lore and scriptures. Nevertheless, there are views to the contrary: "Furthermore, since 95 and 97 percent of the Jewish state was illiterate at the time of Jesus, it must be presumed that Jesus was also illiterate."[22] Of course, we must not equate illiteracy with ignorance. When cultures depend on oral traditions, as did that of Jesus, a high level of sophistication can be achieved without being literate. Still, need we necessarily accept that Jesus could neither read nor write?

Obviously, a determination of the education level of those in first-century Nazareth is difficult if not impossible. Still, "we have reason to think that especially among pious Jews, there existed counterinfluences that would have favored literacy."[23] One such influence would have been the central role of the Torah and the other documents of the Hebrew Bible. As Meier observes: "To be able to be able to read and explain the Scriptures was a revered goal for religiously minded Jews. Hence literacy held special importance for the Jewish community."[24]

None of this proves Jesus could read and write, nor does anything in the Christian scriptures offer proof. Still, if we look at the gospel record in general, Jesus is shown on numerous occasions to be in open debate with those who were certainly literate, the scribes.[25] Yet Jesus never appears to be at a disadvantage. To the contrary, he bests them on every occasion. Even granting that Christians preserved the record, the gospels could reflect the true circumstances. "At any rate, in at least one aspect Jesus was atypical of most men and women of the Greco-Roman world in the 1st century A.D.: he was literate....Jesus comes out of a peasant background, but he is not an ordinary peasant."[26]

D. *The Family Man*

1. HIS PARENTS

Matthew and Luke in their infancy narratives refer to a Joseph, who is regarded as Jesus' father. Mark makes no mention of Joseph and the gospel of John simply identifies Jesus as the "son of Joseph from Nazareth" (1:45; 6:42). There could be several possible explanations for the absence of Joseph during Jesus' public life. A simple one would be that Joseph had died prior to his foster son's meeting with the Baptizer.

In contrast, Mark, Matthew and Luke testify to Jesus' mother being named Mary and affirm her presence during the public life of Jesus. Matthew has Jesus' fellow Nazoreans asking rhetorically, "Is not his mother called Mary?" (13:55). At one point in Mark, Jesus' family, including his mother, comes to fetch him home, apparently concerned for his mental health and for his safety as well (3:31). Finally, John places Jesus' mother at the marriage feast in Cana (2:1) and at the foot of the cross (19:25). The Book of Acts has Mary among those present at Pentecost (1:14). Probably a teenager at his birth, Mary's survival beyond the death of Jesus and even into the days of the early church cannot be discounted as improbable.

2. HIS SIBLINGS

Both Byzantine and Renaissance art picture a "Holy Family" consisting of Jesus, Mary and Joseph. Actually, the gospels present a different picture. In Mark the Nazoreans ask: "Is not this the carpenter, the son of Mary and brother of James and Joses and Judas and Simon, and are not his sisters here with us?" (6:3; see also 3:32). Both Matthew and Luke follow Mark. John preserves the tradition but in a different form. We are told at one point that Jesus "went down to Capernaum with his mother, his brothers, and his disciples; and they remained there a few days" (2:12). Later, his brothers advise him: "Leave here [Galilee] and go to Judea so that your disciples also may see the works you are doing" (7:3). They then precede Jesus in going to Jerusalem (7:10). John adds the startling note: "For not even his brothers believed in him" (7:5). Paul speaks of "James the Lord's brother" and of "the brothers of the Lord" (Gal 1:19; 1 Cor 9:5). As we mentioned earlier, Josephus also refers to a James who is "the brother of Jesus who is called the Messiah."

As to whether these were true siblings of Jesus, Meier concludes: "If—prescinding from faith and later Church teaching—the historian or exegete is asked to render a judgment on the [New Testament] and patristic texts we have examined, viewed simply as historical sources, the most probable opinion is that the brothers and sisters of Jesus were true siblings."[27] For some Christians the question is a delicate one. These hold to a tradition that Jesus' mother bore no children other than Jesus.

Still, if we leave aside the question of their actual parentage,[28] the presence of these "brothers and sisters" gives us a richer view of Jesus' family life. Rather than the sedate scenes so often depicted, Jesus' actual experience was of the hurly-burly life with five brothers and several sisters. His would have been a close-knit family in which family members had to make their own clothes, grow most of their own food and care for several animals.

It was an existence filled from dawn to dusk with the myriad of tasks necessary to survival in those days. Moreover, it would have included the extended family of relatives and in-laws still common in many cultures. Such a family formed the "support group" essential to life in more primitive cultures. For thirty years or so, Jesus lived in a manner not greatly different from his fellow Nazoreans.

3. WAS HE MARRIED?

There is another "family" question that looms for the commentator: Was Jesus married? Even today it would be rare for a mature man in a small Middle Eastern village to remain unmarried. It would have been all the more so with the Jews, who placed such great emphasis on the survival of the people of Israel. It also appears that Jesus' "brothers" and his inner circle of companions were all married men, as we see from Paul: "Do we [himself and Barnabas] not have the right to be accompanied by a believing wife, as do the other apostles and the brothers of the Lord and Cephas?" (1 Cor 9:5). Though Paul was celibate himself, he obviously did not see it as a characteristic of leadership in the Christian communities.

On the other hand, none of the historical records we have or any of the later traditions makes any mention of Jesus having been married. Moreover, Mark, who places great stress on the humanity of Jesus, would hardly have omitted the fact of Jesus' being married. We are brought to the related question: Were there any contemporary examples of such celibacy among the Jews?

As a matter of fact there were. A century and a half before Jesus a Jewish sect appeared, which is known to us as the Essenes (Greek for "pious ones" or "healers"). The ancient documents discovered in 1948 at Qumran are generally regarded as having their origins with this group. About them Meier observes: "As a matter of fact, a Jew from 1st century Palestine (Josephus), a Jew from the 1st century Diaspora [Jews living outside Palestine] (Philo), and a highly educated 1st century pagan (Pliny the Elder) all claimed, in one way or another, that most, if not all, Essenes were celibates."[29] There is no evidence that Jesus was an Essene, but a life of celibacy such as his was not unknown among his contemporaries.

E. The Storyteller

There is an axiom that you can take the boy out of the country, but you cannot take the country out of the boy. For that reason we can find evidence of Jesus' early life in aspects of his public ministry. As C. H. Dodd remarks: "What a singularly complete and convincing picture the parables give of life in a small provincial town—probably a more complete picture of *petit-bourgeois* and peasant life than we possess for any other province of the Roman Empire except Egypt where the papyri come to our aid."[30] Not surprisingly, the stories Jesus told reflected his own experiences of life in Nazareth. Most would agree that "the student of the parables of Jesus…may be confident that he stands on a particularly firm historical foundation."[31]

Reading those parables we can, in our mind's eye, re-create life in the Galilean village of two millennia ago. There is glow of a single lamp illuminating the home (Mk 4:21).[32] Bread rises in preparation for baking (Mt 13:33). Holding a lamp a woman scours her house in search for a lost coin (Lk 15:8). In their single room the household is disturbed by the importuning of a neighbor (Lk 11:7). One's house is a simple structures easily broken into, so burglary is a worry (Mt 24:43).

Not all Nazoreans were in such modest conditions (Lk 12:16). Some could employ slaves (Mk 13:34). These more fortunate ones could put on lavish banquets (Lk 15:23). This may have been particularly true of weddings, when villagers could eat and drink more generously than usual (Mt 22:4).

Outside, in the village marketplace, children play and men idle away the hours waiting for work (Mt 11:16; 20:1–16). Nearby the fields are planted and tilled (Mk 4:3–8, 26–29). Vineyards are tended (Mk 12:1). Sheep and goats are pastured (Mt 18:12–14). Fig trees give their fruit (Mk 13:28). The crops are harvested (Mt 13:30). As with farm communities from time immemorial, life in Nazareth followed the turn of the seasons.

There were times when the routine was broken. A buried treasure is found in a field (Mt 13:44). A widow is able to pester the village magistrate into hearing her plea (Lk 18:1–8). The steward on a nearby estate is found to be an embezzler (Lk 16:1–8). Some men, having contracted to care for a vineyard, attempt to seize it (Mk 12:1–11). Even news of the outside world would have reached out-of-the-way Nazareth (Lk 19:12ff.).[33]

We are told in Matthew that Peter's speech revealed his Galilean origin: "After a little while the bystanders came up and said to Peter, 'Certainly you are also one of them, for your accent betrays you'" (Mt 26:73). The same would have been true for Jesus, where not only his accent but his storytelling clearly marked him as villager, come up from the country. Later we will see other ramifications of Jesus' rural characteristics.

IV. SUMMARY

The Galilee of Jesus' hidden years seemed at peace, but seeds of conflict were stirring to life. Grinding poverty, economic uncertainty, dreams of freedom, all would soon blossom into open revolt later in that first century. Still, before then, Jesus, in the words of Luke "increased in wisdom and in years, and in divine and human favor" (Lk 2:52). He grew up in the midst of family, friends and fellow villagers. Like his father before him, he pursued the trade of woodworker, but there were also animals to care for, most likely a field to cultivate, bartering to do, all the daily tasks that make up peasant life.

The Jesus of history may be, in Meier's words, the "faint outline of a faded fresco," but there was nothing wan or vague about the "real" Jesus. He was part of his world, not set apart from it. Later we will see him almost constantly surrounded by people. This did not mark a change in lifestyle; he had lived that way for thirty years or more. Frequent scenes will show Jesus at table with disciples, friends, even enemies, engaged in the banter that characterizes such gatherings. These were continuations of the "family" meals he had been part of during those "hidden years."

There will be a break with his past when Jesus begins his public ministry, but we must take care not to exaggerate the extent of that rift. Jesus remained to the end what he had been at the beginning, a Galilean. He was also a Jew, and we turn now to that aspect of the Jesus of history.

Chapter Three

JESUS THE JEW

I. THE JEWISH TRAUMA

When I was serving as a campus minister, a student came up to me with an air of discovery. "Father," he said, "Jesus was a Jew!" It is surprising how often Christians fail to appreciate that there is nothing in the New Testament record to indicate that Jesus of Nazareth was anything other than an observant Jew. Such a realization is essential to our understanding of the Jesus of history. Thus crucial to our learning more about Jesus is our knowledge of Jewish religious life in Palestine during the opening years of the first century C.E. It is here that we are presented with a challenge, since between the Judaism of Jesus' day and our own lies a dividing line in Jewish history. In 70 C.E., at the climax of the Jewish War, Jerusalem was razed to the ground and its great Temple destroyed.

It is difficult for us to measure what this catastrophe and it traumatic consequences meant to the Jews. Ever since its rebuilding had begun after the Exile,[1] the Temple had become the focus of the Jewish religion. There and only there could the time-honored sacrifices of ancient Judaism be carried out by the traditional priesthood. The dream of the Jew was to make a pilgrimage, at least once, to the Holy City and offer sacrifice in the Temple.[2] The only parallel to the effect of its destruction would be the upset that would be experienced by the Muslims were the city of Mecca to meet a similar fate.

In the years following 70 C.E., Judaism in the empire underwent a dramatic change. Of the three major Jewish schools of thought mentioned by Josephus,[3] the Pharisees, Sadducees and Essenes, only the Pharisees survived. Eventually they became the dominant influence in the struggle of Judaism to survive the crisis. They determined which documents were to be included in the Hebrew Bible.[4] They collected and preserved the traditional interpretations of the Jewish codes of conduct. Indeed, the existence of Judaism today is testimony to the success of these Pharisaic efforts.

It was not without cost. Those who did not agree with the views of the Pharisees were driven from the synagogues, an understandable if regrettable measure in a time of crisis. Among those expelled were the Jews who had accepted Jesus as the Messiah. There had already been trouble between Jews over the "Christ."[5] The bitterness between the two communities was only exacerbated by the expulsion. As the gospels were written after 70 C.E., they at times reflect the resulting alienation. Sadly, the gospel of John was particularly influenced by the hostility between Christian and Jew as the first century ended.

The upshot is that re-creating the Judaism prior to the disaster of 70 C.E. is difficult and not always possible. The Judaism preserved by the Pharisees as well as the Judaism reflected in the New Testament differ from the Judaism of Jesus' day. Still, there are hints in the gospel record of Jesus' own religious practice and, with care, we can recover something of Jesus, the religious Jew. It is true that Jesus' lifestyle dramatically changed when his public ministry began. Yet some aspects of his later life would have been present during his earlier years as well.

II. JESUS AND JEWISH PIETY

A. The Man of Prayer

From the moment he appears in public, the synoptic gospels present Jesus as a man of prayer. On the day following Jesus' debut in Capernaum (Mk 1:21–27), Mark's gospel tells us: "In the morning, while it was still very dark, he got up and went out to a deserted place, and there he prayed" (1:35). Later, "after saying farewell to [the crowd], [Jesus] went up on the mountain to pray" (6:46). Matthew adds another incident: "Then little children were being brought to him in order that he might lay his hands on them and pray" (19:13). Luke mentions three other occasions on which Jesus prayed (9:18; 11:1; 22:32). Here we can certainly presume that such prayerfulness was a continuation of earlier conduct.

We find in Mark a particularly poignant occasion on which Jesus prayed.

> They went to a place called Gethsemane; and he said to his disciples, "Sit here while I pray." He took with him Peter and James and John, and began to be distressed and agitated. And he said to them, "I am deeply grieved, even to death; remain here, and keep awake." And going a little farther, he threw himself on the ground and prayed that, if it were possible, the hour might pass from him. He said, "Abba, Father, for you all things are possible; remove this cup from me; yet, not what I want, but what you want." (13:32–26; cf. Mt 26:36ff.; Lk 22:31ff.)

Earlier scripture scholars noted the use of the Aramaic *Abba* in the text, a diminutive for "father," similar to "daddy." They thought it indicated something unique to the prayer of Jesus; that is, that he prayed to God with the intimacy of a child. This practice was then handed down to the early Christians (cf. Rom 8:15; Gal 4:6). Yet, charming as that opinion may be, it now seems more likely that Jesus was echoing a custom already found among pious Jews. Speaking of an earlier study, Vermes concludes: "Its literary-historical conclusion, *viz.* that before Jesus Jews did not appeal to God as *Abba,* is not only unproven, but also unlikely."[6] Jesus may not have prayed in a unique way, but certainly, during his life, he prayed in the manner of his contemporaries.

We should also note that, as in the scene in Gethsemane, it appears characteristic of Jesus to pray alone or at a distance from others. In Mark we have: "In the morning, while it was still very dark, he got up and went out to a deserted place, and there he prayed," and "After saying farewell to them, he went up on the mountain to pray (1:35; 6:46). Matthew speaks of another occasion: "And after he had dismissed the crowds, he went up the mountain by himself to pray" (14:23). Luke tells the reader: "But [Jesus] would withdraw to deserted places and pray" (5:16). Such solitary prayer might well have marked Jesus' days in Nazareth.

To the theme of a prayerful Jesus we can add a further note. The synoptics mention Jesus' wearing a "fringed" garment (Mk 6:56; Mt 9:20; 14:36; Lk 8:44). These could well be references to the prayer shawl, characterized by tassels *(tsitsiyot).* As we read in the Book of Numbers: "Speak to the Israelites, and tell them to make fringes on the corners of their garments throughout their generations and to put a blue cord on the fringe at each corner" (15:38). When we imagine Jesus at prayer, we should see him with such a prayer shawl pulled up over his head as would a pious Jew.

B. Jesus and the Synagogue

As Stephen M. Wylen notes: "The origins of the synagogue are shrouded in mystery."[7] Thus we have no exact description of the role of the synagogue in the villages of lower Galilee. Still, the following observation by Wylen would apply to what Jesus experienced: "The primary function of the first century synagogue was for a scholar to read scripture and explain its meaning to the public....The synagogue served as an assembly hall in which the Jewish community would gather to conduct their own affairs."[8] It is not surprising, then, that the gospels show Jesus frequenting the synagogues of Galilee.[9]

Two of these synagogues are singled out, the one in Nazareth and the other in Capernaum.[10] In the former, there is a significant event: "When [Jesus] came to Nazareth, where he had been brought up, he went to the synagogue on the sabbath day, as was his custom. He stood up to read, and the scroll of the prophet Isaiah was given to him" (Lk 4:16–17). Wylen remarks: "Incidentally, Jesus' visit to his hometown is the first instance in recorded history of the custom of Haftarah—reading a selection from the Prophets that relates to the weekly Torah reading."[11] The synagogue certainly played a major role in the religious life of Jesus.

C. Jesus and the Temple

The crowning glory of Judea's capital, Jerusalem, was the great Temple. As note above, it was the presence of the Temple that made the city the focus of first-century Judaism.

> The importance of the Temple extended far beyond the boundaries of the city. Since the reforms of Josiah (621 B.C.), with the centralization of the cultus in Jerusalem on the Deuteronomic pattern, the city was the one holy place for Jews....The Temple of Jerusalem in fact remained the single holy place in the world for Jews. Three times a year pilgrims journeyed there from all over the world.[12]

In the years before his public ministry Jesus would surely have made such pilgrimages from relatively nearby Galilee.

Compressing, as they do, the public life of Jesus into a single year, the synoptic gospels have him coming to Jerusalem only once. Luke, in his infancy narrative, has Jesus brought to the Temple twice, once as an infant and again as a youth (2:22ff.; 41ff.). The gospel of John, in contrast, records five trips to the Holy City. The first and last were at Passover (2:13; 12:12). Other visits took place at the feast of Booths or Sukkoth (7:2–10) and at the feast of the Dedication or Hanukkah (10:22). On a fifth occasion the feast is not identified (51:1).[13] It is generally thought that John's version is the more accurate and, as we noted, would reflect Jesus' behavior prior to his public ministry.

Yet there is a striking omission in the gospel accounts. "It may be worth noting that [Jesus] is nowhere presented as participating in acts of worship."[14] The focus of pilgrimages to the Temple was to offer the traditional animal sacrifices. Yet Jesus is never depicted as doing so, though certainly he must have participated in these rituals on any number of occasions.

The likely reason that the evangelists avoid depicting Jesus before the Temple's altar of sacrifice is that their readers were largely Gentile converts. Their pagan religions had been characterized by animal sacrifices. Paul admonishes the Corinthians not to return to such practices: "I imply that what pagans sacrifice, they sacrifice to demons and not to God. I do not want you to be partners with demons. You cannot drink the cup of the Lord and the cup of demons. You cannot partake of the table of the Lord and the table of demons" (1 Cor 10:20–21). Similarly, the evangelists would be disinclined to record a scene of Jesus participating in such a rituals, even though he did so as a pious Jew.

D. Jesus and the Law

1. THE ROLE OF THE LAW IN JEWISH LIFE

The "codes of conduct," including the Ten Commandments, that we find in the Jewish scriptures (Ex 20–23; Lv 18–20; Dt 21–25) have their roots in rules governing the tribes of the early Israelites. They later augmented and adapted to the period when Israel was a nation. When, after the Exile, the Jews were no longer independent, the Law or Torah became the guide to one's conduct as a Jew. An insight into how the faithful Jew regarded the Law can be seen in Psalms:

The law of the LORD is perfect,
    reviving the soul;
the decrees of the LORD are sure,
    making wise the simple;
the precepts of the LORD are right,
    rejoicing the heart;
the commandment of the LORD is clear,
    enlightening the eyes. (19:7–8)

Happy are those whose way is blameless,
    who walk in the law of the LORD. (119:1)

In time interpretations grew up around the Law designed to adapt its rules to the circumstances in which the Jews found themselves. These accumulated over the centuries, reflecting the different circumstances under which the Jewish people lived. "Torah became the central symbolism of Judaism and summary of what Jews believe and how they live."[15] Sanders affirms that, "on the whole, Jews knew their law extremely well."[16]

After the trauma of 70 C.E., and under the aegis of the Pharisees, these interpretations were collected and codified in the Mishna and the Talmuds. However, we cannot be sure how exactly these records depict the Law as it was observed early in the first century C.E. More precisely, they may not accurately reflect Jewish religious observances in lower Galilee in the same period.

2. JESUS IN CONFLICT WITH THE LAW

It is important to know something of Jesus' own observance of the Law because in his public ministry he is frequently accused of violating Jewish observances. There are, for instance, the breaches of the sabbath rest. This is a serious matter: "Six days shall work be done, but the seventh day is a sabbath of solemn rest, holy to the LORD; whoever does any work on the sabbath day shall be put to death" (Ex 31:15). Yet, on three occasions reported in the synoptics, Jesus heals on the sabbath: the man with a withered hand (Mk 3:1–6; Mt 12:9–14; Lk 6:6–11), a crippled woman (Lk 13:10–17), and a man with dropsy (Lk 14:1–6). Jesus also condones his disciples' violation of the sabbath (Mt 12:1ff.; Lk 6:1). We find a similar criticism of Jesus in John's gospel (5:16; 9:16).

Another violation of proper conduct was Jesus' custom of sharing meals with those designated as "sinners," particularly tax collectors. We read in Mark:

> As he sat at dinner in Levi's house, many tax collectors and sinners were also sitting with Jesus and his disciples—for there were many who followed him. When the scribes of the Pharisees saw that he was eating with sinners and tax collectors, they said to his disciples, "Why does he eat with tax collectors and sinners?" (2:15–16)[17]

Would such conduct have characterized Jesus' life in Nazareth? Would Jesus there have appeared as indifferent to the sabbath rest? Would he have regularly associated with those regarded as unsavory by his fellow Nazoreans? If Jesus' lifestyle was seen as radical in those early days, how can we account for his family's and friends' surprise at his later notoriety? (Mk 6:2–3; Mt 13:54–56). Here may be the roots of a conflict to come.

3. THE URBAN PHARISEES AND THE RURAL JESUS

The gospels show the Pharisees to be the main opponents of Jesus. They were the group Josephus describes as "the most authoritative exponents of the Law."[18] Brown observes, "It may well be that the Pharisees were popular, since the Essenes were too exclusive and the Sadducees too aristocratic; but their support would have been among the well-educated, especially the merchants, traders, and landowners, not among the masses or common laborers."[19] It is safe to say that the strength of the Pharisees lay in the cities, not in the countryside. In fact, at one point we are specifically told that Jesus' opponents came down from Jerusalem (Mk 7:1).

It is hardly unique in human history to note that city dwellers and rural folk tend not to see things in the same light. Jesus' defense of his conduct reflects the rural milieu in which he grew up. In the case of curing the man with the withered hand, Jesus counters his accusers: "Suppose one of you has only one sheep and it falls into a pit on the sabbath; will you not lay hold of it and lift it out? How much more valuable is a human being than a sheep! So it is lawful to do good on the sabbath" (Mt 12:11–12).

Again, when he has cured the crippled woman, Jesus says: "You hypocrites! Does not each of you on the sabbath untie his ox or his donkey from the manger, and lead it away to give it water? And ought not this woman, a daughter of Abraham whom Satan bound for eighteen long years, be set free from this bondage on the sabbath day?" (Lk 13:15–16). In both instances observance of the sabbath rest in Nazareth had to admit for exceptions not encountered in an urban environment. Jesus' city-dwelling challengers might have missed that point.

Similarly, Jesus was quick to defend his companions for doing what may have been common in the fields of lower Galilee: "as they made their way his disciples began to pluck heads of grain" (Mk 2:23). Such a violation might have been excusable in Nazareth, where food was not readily available; in the city it would have been easier to provide in advance for the needs of the sabbath. Jerusalem's Pharisaic "well-educated...merchants, traders, and landowners" could have observed a standard not possible to Jesus and his disciples.

I believer we have a similar situation in understanding Jesus' "table fellowship" with those regarded as "sinners." Jeremias lists those in the "despised trades."[20] Among such are shopkeepers, physicians, butchers, copper smelters, goldsmiths, weavers and barbers, as well as tax collectors. Jeremias points out those who participated in such trades in Jerusalem "were not only despised, nay hated by the people; they were *de jure* deprived of right and ostracized."[21] The "sinners" frequently (some twenty times) mentioned by the evangelists were likely among these unfortunates.

In the city avoiding contact with such "sinners" would have been possible, especially for those better off, like the Pharisees. In a small village such as Nazareth, one wonders just how that could be achieved. There Jesus' associates, friends, even family members could have been engaged in what the Pharisees might have regarded as "despised trade." Later, in his companionship with "sinners," Jesus may have been doing what he had done in the early years. The urban Pharisees may have been scandalized by conduct that was acceptable in Nazareth.

III. SUMMARY

In this chapter and the previous one we have shown that the Jesus of history, during his early years, fit well into the background of Nazareth's village life. Our best evidence of this is the incomprehension of his family when the notoriety of Jesus' public life reached them in Nazareth. Mark notes: "When his family heard it, they went out to restrain him, for people were saying, 'He has gone out of his mind'" (3:21). His friends and neighbors are similarly puzzled. Again Mark writes:

> On the sabbath [Jesus] began to teach in the synagogue, and many who heard him were astounded. They said, "Where did this man get all this? What is this wisdom that has been given to him? What deeds of power are being done by his hands! Is not this the carpenter, the son of Mary and brother of James and Joses and Judas and Simon, and are not his sisters here with us?" And they took offense at him. (6:2–3)

This is not to say that there was nothing seen as unique about Jesus by those who first knew him. I'm sure there was. Yet whatever these qualities were, they were not sufficient to prepare his family, friends and fellow villagers for what was to come. There is the tradition that Jesus himself "was amazed at their unbelief" (Mk 6:6). Apparently his fellow Nazoreans could never overcome their original impression of Jesus.

It may be difficult for the believer to accept that Jesus lived a life so unremarkable for three decades. He was a villager, a family man, an artisan and a pious Jew. There was apparently little to prepare his family, friends and fellow Nazoreans for what is now to happen.

Chapter Four

JESUS AND THE BAPTIZER

I. SOMETHING HAPPENED

In the gospel of Luke the reader is told: "Jesus was about thirty years old when he began his work" (3:22). At a time when people, on average, did not live beyond forty years, Jesus had reached full maturity. As we have seen, he did so among the villagers of lower Galilee. Apparently Jesus was a Nazorean among Nazoreans. As Mary appears to have been a widow, the presumption is that Jesus now headed a large and close-knit family. As such he would now have had considerable responsibilities. Nor would he have been without some significance in the life of his village. Then something happened.

It appears that Jesus was away from Nazareth when news reached his hometown that he was creating a sensation in the villages of lower Galilee. Members of his distraught family, fearing for his sanity, went to fetch Jesus home, only to face rejection (Mk 3:21–34). Later, when Jesus returns to Nazareth, those who had known him all his life were flabbergasted (Mk 6:2–3). Jesus never again returned to his hometown.

The overwhelming evidence is that some traumatic and totally unexpected event occurred during the time Jesus had been away from Nazareth. Otherwise, why did a mature man, an artisan with heavy familial responsibilities, suddenly and apparently without warning abandon his family, his friends and his livelihood? The response in the gospel record is unanimous; it was Jesus' encounter with a well-known contemporary, John the Baptizer.

II. JOHN THE BAPTIZER

A. The World at the Time

The gospel of Luke times the appearance of the Baptizer by citing current events:

> In the fifteenth year of the reign of Emperor Tiberius, when Pontius Pilate was governor of Judea, and Herod was ruler of Galilee, and his brother Philip ruler of the region of Ituraea and Trachonitis, and Lysanias ruler of Abilene, during the high priesthood of Annas and Caiaphas, the word of God came to John son of Zechariah in the wilderness. (3:1–2)

The date was probably around 30 C.E., and Tiberius was ruling the empire from his hideaway on the Isle of Capri. Pontius Pilate was ensconced in Caesarea Maritima, his headquarters on the Mediterranean coast. In the province of Galilee, Herod Antipas with his consort Herodias and her daughter Salome moved from fortress to fortress. To the south, in Jerusalem, the Temple was administered by the priestly family of Annas; his son-in-law Caiaphas was high priest. John the Baptizer was drawing crowds to an area on the eastern side of the Jordan River (Jn 1:28; 10:40).

B. John in History

1. THE BAPTISM OF JOHN

The Jewish historian Josephus comments on the practice that gave John his title:

> For Herod killed [John], although he was a good man and [simply] bade the Jews to join in baptism, provided that they were cultivating virtue and practicing justice toward one another and piety toward God. For [only] thus, in John's opinion, would the baptism [he administered] indeed be acceptable [to God], namely, if they used it to obtain not pardon for some sins but rather the cleansing of their bodies, inasmuch as [it was taken for granted that] their souls had already been purified by justice.[1]

In Josephus's view the baptismal ritual was symbolic of a commitment to a life of virtue and justice. It did not actually obtain pardon for sin. The rite, however, was not unique to John.

The Greek means simply "to dip," though "into water" is usually implied.[2] Religious rituals involving symbolic washing are found in many cultures and Judaism was no exception (Lv 14:5–6, 50–52; Nm 19:13, 20–21). The Essene community at Qumran, thought to be the source of the Dead Sea scrolls, employed such symbolic bathings frequently. The proximity of the Qumran locale to where John is supposed to have been active is thought by some to be significant. In contrast John appears to have baptized a person only once. Moreover, though John had followers (Acts 18:25; 19:1–4), his baptism was not an initiation ceremony as it became later in both the Jewish and Christian communities.[3]

2. HIS APPEARANCE

The gospels add to the picture of John. However, as we will see, that record must be used with care since it inevitably reflects the Christian evaluation of John in relation to Jesus. Moreover, we have again to keep in mind our distinction between "prophecy historicized" and "history remembered." For instance, Mark describes the Baptizer as follows: "Now John was clothed with camel's hair, with a leather belt around his waist, and he ate locusts and wild honey" (1:6). Since Mark presents John as a prophet (11:32), the description could simply be reinforcing this view by reflecting what had been said of the prophets in the Hebrew Bible (2 Kgs 1:8; Zec 13:4). On the other hand, details of the unusual lifestyle of a well-known figure could easily have been preserved in the popular memory.

John's somewhat bizarre appearance fits well the locale of his activity. Mark relates that "John the baptizer appeared in the wilderness" (1:4). A Q tradition refers to John's being in the wilderness (Mt 11:7; Lk 7:24). John's activity in the desert region on the eastern side of the Jordan, as reported in the gospels (Mk 1:5; Mt 3:6; Lk 3:3; Jn 10:40), would qualify as a wilderness. However, Mark may have been influenced by the quotation from Isaiah he uses to introduce John to his readers as "the voice of one crying out in the wilderness: 'Prepare the way of the Lord, make his paths straight'" (Mk 1:3; Is 40:3).

Of course, the region on the eastern side of the Jordan was also a place with great significance in the history of Israel. From there the Israelites, under the leadership of Joshua, began their conquest of Canaan, the promised land. It might also be possible that John himself chose to draw people out to a desertlike area beyond the Jordan to call to their minds those ideal Israelites of old who had begun their conquest of the promised land from the same locale. It is not easy to determine how much of the passage is "history remembered" and how much "prophecy historicized."

3. JOHN'S MESSAGE

As we saw above, Josephus described John's message as one of "cultivating virtue and practicing justice toward one another and piety toward God." Turning to the gospels, the Q source gives us the following:

> But when [John] saw many Pharisees and Sadducees coming for baptism, he said to them, "You brood of vipers! Who warned you to flee from the wrath to come? Bear fruit worthy of repentance. Do not presume to say to yourselves, 'We have Abraham as our ancestor'; for I tell you, God is able from these stones to raise up children to Abraham. Even now the ax is lying at the root of the trees; every tree therefore that does not bear good fruit is cut down and thrown into the fire." (Mt 3:7–10)

In Luke 3:7–9 the message is not addressed to specific groups, as in Matthew, but simply to "the crowds." In the light of Josephus's account, there is no overwhelming reason for supposing these words did not originate with the Baptizer himself.

John's basic theme is the urgency to reform, to "bear fruit" before a calamity occurs. The language is reminiscent of Isaiah (Is 10:33–34; 32:19), and the warning is a prophetic theme. Israel's failure to return to God will bring on disaster. Yet, as Meier points out: "What is striking, therefore, is that the threat of the sermon…is directed at ordinary Jews who have taken the trouble to come out to John to be baptized. It is to them, to the ostensibly well disposed, that John utters this withering denunciation."[4] Such warnings "prompt many authors to speak of John as an 'apocalyptic' [Greek: *apokalupsis,* "revelation"] figure."[5] Whatever the content of John's preaching, its eloquence and power had tragic results.

4. HIS DEATH

a. As Reported in Josephus

By way of background, Herod Antipas was married to the daughter of Aretas, the Nabatean ruler, but he abandoned her to marry Herodias, who had been the wife of his half-brother. As a result of this, his former father-in-law made war on Antipas and defeated him 37 C.E. In the following quotation from the *Antiquities,* Josephus tells of Jews who believed the defeat was actually a punishment for Antipas's execution of John:

> But to some of the Jews it seemed that the army of Herod was destroyed by God—indeed, God quite justly punishing [Herod] to avenge what he had done to John, who was surnamed the Baptist....
>
> And when the others [namely, ordinary Jews] gathered together [around John]—for their excitement reached fever pitch as they listened to [his] words—Herod began to fear that John's powerful ability to persuade people might lead to some sort of revolt, for they seemed likely to do whatever he counseled. So [Herod] decided to do away with John by a preemptive strike, before he sparked a revolt. Herod considered this a better [course of action] than to wait until the situation changed and [then] to regret [his delay] when he was engulfed by a crisis.
>
> And so, because of Herod's suspicion, John was sent in chains to Machaerus, the mountain fortress previously mentioned; there he was killed. But the Jews were of the opinion that the army was destroyed to avenge John, God wishing to inflict harm on Herod.[6]

Thus Josephus preserves the tradition that it was the effectiveness of John's oratory that brought him to the attention of Herod Antipas. Someone who could gather large crowds was an implied threat to those in power. In the light of the disaster that befell Palestine as the result of rabble-rousers some thirty years later, Herod's trepidations were not unfounded.

b. As Reported in Mark

The author of the first gospel preserved another tradition about the death of John. The basic facts are the same, though Herod's motive for the execution differs:

> For Herod himself had sent men who arrested John, bound him, and put him in prison on account of Herodias, his brother Philip's wife, because Herod had married her. For John had been telling Herod, "It is not lawful for you to have your brother's wife." And Herodias had a grudge against him, and wanted to kill him. But she could not, for Herod feared John, knowing that he was a righteous and holy man, and he protected him. When he heard him, he was greatly perplexed; and yet he liked to listen

to him. But an opportunity came when Herod on his birthday gave a banquet for his courtiers and officers and for the leaders of Galilee. When the daughter of Herodias came in and danced, she pleased Herod and his guests; and the king said to the girl, "Ask me for whatever you wish, and I will give it." And he solemnly swore to her, "Whatever you ask me, I will give you, even half of my kingdom." She went out and said to her mother, "What should I ask for?" She replied, "The head of John the baptizer." Immediately she rushed back to the king and requested, "I want you to give me at once the head of John the Baptist on a platter." The king was deeply grieved; yet out of regard for his oaths and for the guests, he did not want to refuse her. Immediately the king sent a soldier of the guard with orders to bring John's head. He went and beheaded him in the prison, brought his head on a platter, and gave it to the girl. Then the girl gave it to her mother. When his disciples heard about it, they came and took his body, and laid it in a tomb. (6:17–29)

It is easy to see why the Marcan tradition, replete with all the juicy details, was preserved. Indeed, it has remained popular with artists down through the centuries, even inspiring a play and an opera in modern times.

It should be noted that the Marcan version has touches in the fate of John that resemble that of Jesus: a reluctant ruler is forced to decree an unjust execution on an innocent man. The preservation in two ancient documents of the traditions concerning his death serves to emphasize the prominence of John, before and after his death. That death would have taken place shortly after Jesus began his public life, as we see in Mark: "Now after John was arrested, Jesus came to Galilee, proclaiming the good news of God" (1:14). That would place John's demise not long after 27 or 28 C.E.

III. JOHN THE APOCALYPTIC

A. *Apocalyptics in Palestine*

Cartoonists have frequently focused on an isolated figure, usually bearded, wearing a robe and carrying a sign reading THE END IS NEAR! Such is the "apocalyptic" in the popular imagination. Actually such "prophets of doom" do tend to make their appearance at times of social stress. Humorous to some, they are taken seriously by others.

The latter would have been true of many Jews at the time of John. The regime of Pilate was a tumultuous one. On his arrival in Jerusalem to take up his role as procurator, he sought to place the army's standards where they would overlook the Temple, an action that nearly resulted in open revolt. Then, seeking to build a new aqueduct, Pilate decided to raid the Temple treasury. In the riot that resulted thousands were said to have died. Luke mentions a further incident in which others were killed by the procurator (13:1). Eventually, owing to the severity of his rule, Pilate was recalled to Rome in disgrace.

Added to the results of Pilate's conduct would have been the general unrest in Judea stemming from Rome's oppressive rule, a rule that cruelly must have dashed any hope for freedom. Some chose the course of violent revolt. Others, like John, looked to the God of Israel and to a cosmic intervention that would restore the independence Judea had known in the previous century. "It may therefore be more accurate to describe John as an eschatological prophet tinged with some apocalyptic motifs."[7]

B. The Apocalyptic in the Gospels

Matthew maintains the apocalyptic mood in the warning of John: "Even now the ax is lying at the root of the trees; every tree therefore that does not bear good fruit is cut down and thrown into the fire" (3:10). Luke, in contrast, focuses on moral reform:

And the crowds asked him, "What then should we do?" In reply he said to them, "Whoever has two coats must share with anyone who has none; and whoever has food must do likewise." Even tax collectors came to be baptized, and they asked him, "Teacher, what should we do?' He said to them, "Collect no more than the amount prescribed for you." Soldiers also asked him, "And we, what should we do?" He said to them, "Do not extort money from anyone by threats or false accusation, and be satisfied with your wages." (3:10–14)

The difference is not contradictory: "John would have been a most unusual spiritual guide within Judaism at the turn of the era if he had not delivered some teaching on morality and daily conduct."[8] Yet such a call to a higher ethical standard is not the usual apocalyptic fare. The latter is usually a demand for some radical action in the face of a coming calamity.

IV. THE ENCOUNTER BETWEEN JOHN AND JESUS

A. An Embarrassment

It is usually taken for granted that John encountered Jesus when the latter presented himself for baptism. Yet the historical evidence for such a meeting is slim. Josephus, who mentions both figures, does not record that they ever met. Mark, followed by Matthew, originates the report that they met. Luke does not directly identify who baptized Jesus (3:21) and the gospel of John omits the tradition of John's baptizing Jesus. In the face of such a lack of corroboration, one would usually be skeptical about the actuality of the event.

If the encounter between John and Jesus did not occur, it would mean that the earliest Christians invented the story. There would be ample motive for doing so. John was undoubtedly a famous personage. Josephus preserves the view that Herod was punished by God for John's execution. In the Marcan account John heroically defends God's law. And there is evidence that followers of John were active in the early days of Christianity (Acts 18:25; 19:3).

In contrast, Jesus is executed as a common criminal for sedition. Moreover, he is shown to have been abandoned by his immediate followers, even betrayed by one of them. All in all, associating Jesus with John at the time of the former's radical change in lifestyle would recommend itself.

That argument, however, is undermined by the persistent and extensive efforts of the gospels to show the superiority of Jesus over John (see below). It appears that rather than inventing the encounter by these two contemporaries, the early Christians were embarrassed by it. "As a matter of plain fact, the gospels do evince embarrassment at the story of Jesus' baptism and try to do 'damage control' as best they can."[9] If Jesus' involvement with John could not be denied, it could be given a "spin" that made Jesus appear superior.

B. One Who Is to Follow

The *Q* tradition in the gospels preserves the prediction of the Baptizer that he will be followed by another apocalyptic figure:

I baptize you with water for repentance, but one who is more powerful than I is coming after me; I am not worthy to carry his sandals. He will baptize you with the Holy Spirit and fire. His winnowing fork is in his hand, and he will clear his threshing floor and will gather his wheat into the granary; but the chaff he will burn with unquenchable fire. (Mt 3:11–12; see also Lk 3:16)

Some of these words are also found elsewhere: "The one who is more powerful than I is coming after me; I am not worthy to stoop down and untie the thong of his sandals. I have baptized you with water; but he will baptize you with the Holy Spirit" (Mk 1:7; see also Acts 13:25; Jn 1:26–27, 33). "Hence, we have good reason to accept this as substantially the Baptist's own teaching."[10] But who is John's "one who is more powerful than I?" The reference may have been intentionally vague: "In other words, John did expect some further agent of God who would bring the eschatological drama to its proper denouement, but he had no clear idea who that would be."[11]

The followers of Jesus, aware of the Baptizer's prophecy, identified Jesus as the figure John predicted. The Fourth Gospel is explicit. The Baptizer himself says of Jesus: "This is he of whom I said, 'After me comes a man who ranks ahead of me because he was before me'" (1:30). Less direct, but still subordinating John, *Q* has a passage where John, while imprisoned, sends his disciples to question Jesus (Mt 11:2; Lk 7:18–19). Jesus praises John profusely, but with a crucial limitation: "Truly I tell you, among those born of women no one has arisen greater than John the Baptist; yet the least in the kingdom of heaven is greater than he" (Mt 11:11; Lk 7:28).

C. The Theophany

In Mark and the other synoptics there is a heavenly affirmation of Jesus at the time of his baptism:

And just as [Jesus] was coming up out of the water, he saw the heavens torn apart and the Spirit descending like a dove on him. And a voice came from heaven, "You are my Son, the Beloved; with you I am well pleased." (Mk 1:10–11; see Mt 3:17; Lk 3:22)

The passage appears to be a reference to the prophecy of Isaiah:

The spirit of the LORD shall rest on him,
  the spirit of wisdom and understanding,
  the spirit of counsel and might,
  the spirit of knowledge and the fear of the LORD....
Here is my servant, whom I uphold,
  my chosen, in whom my soul delights;
I have put my spirit upon him;
  he will bring forth justice to the nations....
The spirit of the LORD God is upon me,
  because the LORD has anointed me;
  he has sent me to bring good news to the oppressed,
  to bind up the brokenhearted,
  to proclaim liberty to the captives,
  and release to the prisoners. (11:2; 42:1; 61:1)

One of the psalms may also be a reference:

I will tell of the decree of the LORD:
He said to me, "You are my son;
  today I have begotten you." (2:7)

Similarly, we have the opening line of Ezekiel: "In the thirtieth year, in the fourth month, on the fifth day of the month, as I was among the exiles by the river Chebar, the heavens were opened, and I saw visions of God" (Ez 1:1).

In the light of these references Meier concludes: "To sum up, then, the message of the theophany: the Son of God, the Royal Davidic Messiah, is anointed with God's spirit to be the final prophet and servant of the Lord sent to a sinful people."[12] In the glow of that revelation the Baptizer would seem to fade into insignificance. Rather than Jesus being enhanced by John's presence, the reverse is true.

D. Jesus Transcending John

Matthew, not content with the above, adds that the Baptizer himself recognizes the superiority of Jesus:

John would have prevented him, saying, "I need to be baptized by you, and do you come to me?" But Jesus answered him, "Let it be so now; for it is proper for us in this way to fulfill all righteousness." Then he consented. (3:14–15)

It is only at Jesus' insistence that he is baptized by John. Again, the relative importance of the two figures is reversed from what one would expect if John were regarded as superior to Jesus.

Luke presents a more elaborate framework with which to indicate the priority of Jesus over John. He provides an infancy narrative for the Baptist wherein John and Jesus are relatives, possibly cousins. The birth of each is announced by an angel. However, the reactions of the parents are sharply contrasted. Zechariah doubts and is struck dumb. Mary gives her unqualified consent: "Here am I, the servant of the Lord; let it be with me according to your word" (Lk 1:38). Later, when Mary visits John's mother, both pregnant, the priority of Jesus over John is stressed. "When Elizabeth heard Mary's greeting, the child leaped in her womb.... [She said:] 'And why has this happened to me, that the mother of my Lord comes to me?'" (Lk 1:41, 43). Though they are blood relatives, Jesus is carefully shown to be superior to John.

Luke, after very briefly mentioning John's imprisonment by Herod, tells the reader: "Now when all the people were baptized, and when Jesus also had been baptized and was praying, the heaven was opened" (3:19–21). There is no mention of John actually baptizing Jesus. The impression is one of glossing over the event rather than emphasizing it.

As for the Fourth Gospel, there is no reference to John baptizing Jesus. How could there be? Jesus is presented to the reader in the most exalted language, indicating his Divinity: "In the beginning was the Word, and the Word was with God, and the Word was God" (1:1). John does echo a passage from the earlier account of the baptism: "I saw the Spirit descending from heaven like a dove, and it remained on him" (1:32). The purpose of the vision, however, is to reveal to the Baptizer the identity of Jesus. Indeed, as we have seen, John himself testifies to the transcendence of Jesus: "This is he of whom I said, 'After me comes a man who ranks ahead of me because he was before me'" (1:30).

E. Was Jesus a Disciple of John?

We can accept that Jesus did encounter John the Baptizer and did submit to the ritual that characterized the latter's ministry. However, might there have been more than a transitory encounter between the two contemporaries? The synoptic accounts rule out that possibility, since after appearing suddenly on the bank of the Jordan River and being baptized, we read in Mark: "The Spirit immediately drove him out into the wilderness" (Mk 1:12).

There is in the Fourth Gospel, however, a hint of a more complex relationship between Jesus and John. Again Jesus is introduced abruptly at the scene of John's ministry (Jn 1:29), but in John's account there is no mention Jesus being baptized and thus no explanation for his presence where John was baptizing across the Jordan. The only others on the scene are John's adversaries or his disciples (1:19, 35). Not an adversary, the implication is that Jesus too was a disciple.

Moreover, Jesus' own original disciples appear to have been drawn from among the Baptizer's followers (1:38–39). These would be Andrew and Philip and, possibly, Peter and Nathanael. "Yet when all the Johannine theology is stripped away, an embarrassing and surprising fact remains—a fact one would have never guessed from the Synoptic presentation: Some of the disciples of Jesus first gave their allegiance to the Baptist, and only after a while transferred it to Jesus, whom they first met in the Baptist's circle."[13] Were Jesus also a follower of John, his recruiting his own followers from the same group would seem logical.

Finally, there is evidence of a relationship between Jesus' ministry and that of John. We read in the Fourth Gospel that at one point the Baptizer is told: "Rabbi, the one who was with you across the Jordan, to whom you testified, here he is baptizing, and all are going to him" (3:26). A few verses later the gospel denies that Jesus baptized, though his disciples did (4:2). Whatever the truth, it is possible that after separating from John, Jesus continued what appeared to be a rival ministry.

V. SUMMARY

Meier observes: "In my opinion, Jesus' being baptized by John is one of the most historically certain events ascertainable by any reconstruction of the historical Jesus."[14] It might reasonably be held that Jesus remained with John for a time and then separated from his mentor, taking with him the first of those who would be called apostles. That more gradual transition makes more understandable the dramatic change Jesus underwent. That change is aptly characterized as follows:

> At the very least, Jesus' baptism meant a fundamental break in his life; baptism as watershed. As far as our meager sources allow us to know, before his baptism by John, Jesus was a respectable, unexceptional, and unnoticed woodworker in Nazareth. Both family and neighbors were shocked and offended by Jesus once he undertook his ministry, and not without reason. Apparently there was nothing in his previous life that foreshadowed or ostensibly prepared for his decision to dedicate himself totally to a religious mission to all Israel, a mission lacking any official sanction.[15]

The Jesus of history may owe more to the Baptizer than history itself has recorded.

Chapter Five

JESUS, THE CHARISMATIC SAGE

I. THE SPAN OF JESUS' PUBLIC MINISTRY

A. *The Beginning*

The gospel of Luke indicates the "when" of Jesus' emergence into the light of history as follows. I have inserted the pertinent dates following Meier:[1]

> In the fifteenth year of the reign of Emperor Tiberius [who reigned as sole emperor 14–37 C.E.], when Pontius Pilate was governor of Judea [26–36 C.E.], and Herod was ruler of Galilee [ruled 4 B.C.E.–39 C.E.], and his brother Philip ruler of the region of Ituraea and Trachonitis [4 B.C.E.–33/34 C.E.], and Lysanias ruler of Abilene [dates unknown], during the high priesthood of Annas and Caiaphas [Caiaphas was high priest 18–36 C.E.], the word of God came to John son of Zechariah in the wilderness. He went into all the region around the Jordan, proclaiming a baptism of repentance for the forgiveness of sins. (3:1–3)

At the time of his encounter with John, Jesus was not a young man but a mature adult. "Hence Jesus was probably in his early to mid-thirties at the beginning of his ministry and in his mid- to late thirties at its conclusion."[2]

B. *How Long Was Jesus' Public Ministry?*

Mark's gospel (followed by Matthew and Luke) indicates a ministry of one year, climaxed by Jesus' sole visit to Jerusalem (11ff.). In sharp contrast, John's gospel presents a three-year ministry with two visits to Jerusalem at Passover, the latter, of course, his final visit (2:13; 12:12); a visit for the feast of Booths and another for Hanukkah (7:2-10;

10:22); and a fifth visit for an unidentified feast (5:1). John recounts that Jesus spent another Passover on the shore of the Sea of Galilee (6:4). Can we make any judgment as to which of these presentations reflects more accurately the span of Jesus' public life?

It is possible that the traditions reflected in the synoptic gospels condense the events of Jesus' ministry in order to focus on the single Passover when that ministry came to its dramatic conclusion. Indeed, the almost frenetic pace of Mark appears unrealistic. Though Matthew and Luke have expanded the amount of material, they have the same structure. In the light of this most scholars would tend to favor the Johannine chronology. "If we ask what *minimum* length of time the Gospel [John's] narrative *demands,* the answer must be two years, plus a month or two."[3]

The biographer usually seeks to arrange for the reader the sequence of events in his subject's life. Unfortunately, in our search it will not be possible to do so. We have Meier's observation: "We must constantly remind ourselves of the basic rule: between Jesus' baptism and the last week of [Jesus'] life, there is no before or after. The time frame and plot line of each evangelist are his own creation."[4] Where, under the usual circumstances, a chronology gives us a sense of development in a person, there is none of that for the Jesus of history. Moreover, each evangelist, incorporating differing traditions and writing for differing readerships, presents a distinct portrait of Jesus suited to his particular purposes. Our challenges is to see if, behind these versions, we can detect that "faded fresco" of a Jesus fitting into the milieu of early-first-century lower Galilee.

II. THE SAGE

In understanding any historical personage it is most helpful if there are others at the time who are comparable to the one being studied. Jesus of Nazareth was, of course, unique in many ways, but he may also have fitted into the pattern of other contemporary figures.

In his study of the *Q* source Burton L. Mack has a section entitled "The Original Book of *Q*."[5] The passages he quotes are said to be an early collection of Jesus' sayings, his wise advice. Many of the passages Mack cites are from the following section of Luke:

> But I say to you that listen, Love your enemies, do good to those who hate you, bless those who curse you, pray for those who abuse you. If anyone strikes you on the cheek, offer the other also; and from anyone who takes away your coat do not withhold even your shirt. Give to everyone who begs from you; and if anyone takes away your goods, do not ask for them again. Do to others as you would have them do to you.
>
> If you love those who love you, what credit is that to you? For even sinners love those who love them. If you do good to those who do good to you, what credit is that to you? For even sinners do the same. If you lend to those from whom you hope to receive, what credit is that to you? Even sinners lend to sinners, to receive as much again. But love your enemies, do good, and lend, expecting nothing in return. Your reward will be great, and you will be children of the Most High; for he is kind to the ungrateful and the wicked. Be merciful, just as your Father is merciful.
>
> Do not judge, and you will not be judged; do not condemn, and you will not be condemned. Forgive, and you will be forgiven; give, and it will be given to you. A good measure, pressed down, shaken together, running over, will be put into your lap; for the measure you give will be the measure you get back.
>
> He also told them a parable: "Can a blind person guide a blind person? Will not both fall into a pit? A disciple is not above the teacher, but everyone who is fully qualified will be like the teacher. Why do you see the speck in your neighbor's eye, but do not notice the log in your own eye? Or how can you say to your neighbor, "Friend, let me take out the speck in your eye,' when you yourself do not see the log in your own eye? You hypocrite, first take the log out of your own eye, and then you will see clearly to take the speck out of your neighbor's eye."
>
> No good tree bears bad fruit, nor again does a bad tree bear good fruit; for each tree is known by its own fruit. Figs are not gathered from thorns, nor are grapes picked from a bramble bush. The good person out of the good treasure of the heart produces good, and the evil person out of evil treasure produces evil; for it is out of the abundance of the heart that the mouth speaks. (6:27–45)

Among the parables told by Jesus we also find those that could be the advice of a wise teacher. From Luke we have the true meaning of love of neighbor expounded in the story of the Good Samaritan (10:25–37).

There is the advice to persist in prayer in the stories of the friend asking for help at night and of the unjust judge ultimately prevailed upon by the poor widow (11:5–8; 18:1–8). The Prodigal Son parable is actually about God's unlimited forgiveness (15:11–32). The Pharisee and the publican story contrasts God's responses to self-serving prayer and to selfless prayer (18:9–14).

The above examples, and many more found the gospel record, give us the picture of a wise man moving about the villages and small towns of lower Galilee, catching the attention of his hearers by vivid language and stories. It is not hard to see why Jesus of Nazareth gathered a crowd and even some followers who would form a small entourage. However, there was much more to Jesus than that.

III. THE CHARISMATIC

A. Background

There are other counterparts to Jesus as we see in the following suggestion made by Vermes:

> He [Jesus] was a healer, the physician par excellence....In consequence, if his religious personality is to be reconstructed and his affinities with the spiritual trends of his time determined, the three fundamental aspects of his function must be examined in their natural setting. His roles, that is to say, as healer of the physically ill, exorciser of the possessed, and dispenser of forgiveness to sinners must be seen in the context in which they belong, namely charismatic Judaism. It is not until he is placed within that stream, in the company of other religious personalities with affiliations to diverse movements and groups, that his work and personality can be seen in true perspective and proportion.[6]

A charismatic figure is one displaying special powers arising from sources beyond the ordinary. In the religious sense, the source is God. "The representation of Jesus as a man whose supernatural abilities derived, not from secret powers, but from immediate contact with God, proves him to be a genuine charismatic, the true heir of an age-old prophetic religious line."[7] We have two other examples of charismatic Judaism.

B. Two Jewish Charismatics

1. HONI THE CIRCLEDRAWER

Honi the Circledrawer lived in Judea prior to its conquest by Pompey in 63 B.C.E. He received his title from a Jewish story about his praying for rain. Frustrated by God's failure to answer his petition, Honi drew a circle on the ground and refused to move from it until the rains came. His insistent importuning succeeded. However, some felt that Honi's action, though effective, was impertinent to the point of blasphemy.[8]

Though we have no record of Jesus' acting in the manner of Honi, we do have two instances when Jesus recommended insistence in prayer. These are the parables of the man demanding bread from a neighbor and of the widow demanding justice from the corrupt official (Lk 11:5ff.; 18:2ff.). The concluding remark of Jesus in the latter parable resembles the insistence of Honi: "And will not God grant justice to his chosen ones who cry to him day and night? Will he delay long in helping them?" (Lk 18:7).

2. HANINA BEN DOSA

Hanina ben Dosa brings us closer to Jesus. He too was a Galilean and is said to have been born not many miles from Nazareth, but perhaps a generation later than Jesus. One tradition concerning Hanina is of particular interest. We are told that the son of the famed rabbi Gamaliel[9] had fallen seriously ill. A delegation from Jerusalem was sent to Hanina, already famed as a healer. Hanina went alone to pray and on returning told the petitioners that the child was cured. Skeptical, they carefully noted the time. On their return to the Holy City they learned that the boy had recovered at the exact hour Hanina had prayed.

Hanina is particularly important in our search. "Nevertheless, the hypothesis associating charismatic Judaism with Galilee acquires further support in the incontestably Galilean background of Hanina ben Dosa, one of the most important figures for understanding of the charismatic stream in the first century A.D."[10] The resemblance between Jesus and the charismatic Hanina is reflected in Hanina's cure, at a distance, of Gamaliel's child, and Jesus' similar cure of the centurion's slave (Mt 8:5ff.).[11]

C. *The Hasidim*

Vermes adds this note:

> One of the prime characteristics of the ancient Hasidim or devout is that their prayer was believed to be all-powerful, capable of performing miracles.…It is, in any case, safe and justifiable to conclude that the unsophisticated religious ambiance of Galilee was apt to produce holy men of the Hasidic type."[12]

It is doubtful that the Hasidim mentioned by Vermes are related to the group referred to in either 1 Maccabees 2:42 or 2 Maccabees 14:6. An Hasid may simply have been one regarded as extraordinarily pious.

IV. THE HASIDIM *VS.* THE PHARISEES

A. *Rural* vs. *Urban*

We have already noted that some of the tension between Jesus and the Pharisees stemmed from the differing attitudes of a lower Galilean villager and the more urbane Jerusalemites. In addition, the largely rural Galileans, far from the more erudite environs of Judea and Jerusalem, responded more readily to the charismatic Hasidim. These "pious ones" were at odds with the Pharisees. Vermes cites two sources for the alienation:

> The first, though perhaps less important, lies in the Hasidic refusal to conform in matters of behavior and religious observance. The second reason springs from the threat posed by the unrestrained authority of the charismatic to the upholders of the established religious order.[13]

If it is true as Vermes notes that "Jesus of Nazareth would seem very much at home in such company [the Hasidim],"[14] then this would only serve to further exacerbate the tension between Jesus and the Pharisees. This is borne out to some degree by the gospel record, where Jesus and the Pharisees are shown to be at loggerheads for the very reasons Vermes cites: his "refusal to conform" and his "unrestrained authority."

In chapter 3 we discussed Jesus' attitude toward the Law and his conflict with the Pharisees over it. Again and again the Pharisees take a "law and order" stance against Jesus for his seeming indifference to accepted behavior. There is the question of fasting, the violations of the

Sabbath rest and the omission of ritual washings (Mk 2:18; 2:24; 3:2; 7:5). Like the Hasidim, Jesus may have been rather cavalier in his attitude toward the Law. He was certainly more liberal in his application of the Torah when compared to the strict observance of the Pharisees. Traditionally, charismatics tend to place little emphasis on conforming to rules, religious or otherwise. Again, viewing the Jesus of history against his a rural background will help us to understand more clearly some aspects of the gospel record.[15]

B. "By Whose Authority?"

At root, of course, it comes down to a question of authority. Jesus' opponents appeal to their pedigree as scholars and their association with Jerusalem as the center of Jewish religious life. Jesus, the rural Hasid, lacked such prestigious credentials. Thus, as Mark records: "They were astounded at [Jesus'] teaching, for he taught them as one having authority, and not as the scribes" (1:22). At his trial Jesus is questioned on this very point: "By what authority are you doing these things? Who gave you this authority to do them?" (11:28) How could Jesus' justify what he said and did? Vermes states, "The charismatics' informal familiarity with God and confidence in the efficacy of their words was also deeply disliked by those whose authority derived from established channels."[16] When, in prayer, Jesus addresses God as Abba (Mk 14:36), he displays just such familiarity. Those who drew their prestige from "established channels" were unlikely to look kindly upon one who challenged their authority with an authority of his own.

V. CONCLUSION

How far can we carry this picture of Jesus as a "pious one"? As already noted, there was nothing out of the ordinary about Jesus' life prior to his encounter with John the Baptizer.[17] What changed? We may have a clue in the short passage found in Mark: "And the Spirit immediately drove [Jesus] out into the wilderness. He was in the wilderness forty days, tempted by Satan; and he was with the wild beasts; and the angels waited on him" (Mk 1:12–13). We have more elaborate versions in Matthew and Luke (Mt 4:1ff.; Lk 4:1ff.). The forty days are certainly a reference to the forty-year preparation of Israel in the desert before reentering the promised land, that is, "prophecy historicized." But behind the event might well have been a period of solitude, one ending, according to Mark, with the arrest of the Baptizer (1:14).

In summary, Jesus of Nazareth, drawn to the charismatic Baptizer (also an Hasid?), undergoes a profound religious experience. He then begins a period of living in solitude. From this he emerges a changed man. There may have a time when he was a disciple of John's. But at some point he comes into his own, now a charismatic sage. Regarded as a "pious one," he moves through lower Galilee with a small group of followers.

However, there was a further dimension to these Hasidim. Speaking of Jesus, Vermes observed, as noted above: "His roles, that is to say, as healer of the physically ill, exorciser of the possessed, and dispenser of forgiveness to sinners must be seen in the context in which they belong, namely charismatic Judaism." These remarkable roles and actions are attributed to Jesus. Indeed, they are at the core of the gospels. We turn to them now.

Chapter Six

JESUS, THE MAN OF DEED

I. THE MIRACLE AND THE MODERN MIND

A. *Introduction*

Vermes points out that the miracle-working Hasidim are called "men of deed."[1] As we just seen, remarkable accomplishments were attributed to both Honi the Circledrawer and Hanina ben Dosa. Josephus spoke of Jesus as "a doer of startling deeds."[2] In Luke we read: "Jesus of Nazareth, who was a prophet mighty in deed and word before God and all the people" (Lk 24:19). How is the historian to evaluate the traditions that claim that Jesus did in fact work miracles? They present a particular challenge in our search for the Jesus of history.

Though a considerable majority of Americans accept the possibility of divine intervention in human affairs, historians tend to remain skeptical.[3] As an example, Crossan has no problem with a blanket dismissal of Jesus' miracles. He speaks of him as one "who did not and could not cure that disease (leprosy) or any other."[4] Any consideration of the Jesus of history must treat the question of the miraculous.

B. *The Miracle*

The American Heritage Dictionary definition of *miracle* is "an event that appears unexplainable by the laws of nature and so is held to be supernatural in origin or an act of God." When one speaks of something as "unexplainable by the laws of nature," the existence of such "laws" is implied. Uniformity and regularity in natural phenomena are presumed in today's worldview. Thus activities like walking on water, feeding thousands with a few loaves and fishes, and turning water into wine would be considered "unexplainable by the laws of nature." Now, if one believed that such violations of the laws of nature were impossible, then the report of a miracle would either be discounted or given an explanation. Failing the latter, the event would be attributed to something in the nature of things not yet discovered.[5]

However, even if a miracle is regarded as *possible,* another criterion must be met. As we saw in the definition above, the occurrence must be "held to be supernatural in origin or an act of God." Meier feels that this is crucial and introduces a limitation to a historical evaluation:

> The historian can ascertain whether an extraordinary event has taken place in a religious setting, whether someone has claimed it to be a miracle, and—if there is enough evidence—whether a human action, physical forces in the universe, misperception, illusion, or fraud can explain the event. If all these explanations are excluded, the historian may conclude that an event claimed by some people to be miraculous has no reasonable explanation or adequate cause in any human activity or physical force. To go beyond that judgment and to affirm *either* that God has directly acted to bring about this startling event *or* that God has not done so is to go beyond what any historian can affirm in his or her capacity as a historian and to enter the domain of philosophy or theology."[6]

C. Jesus and the Miracle

In examining the record of Jesus' "startling deeds" the historian can conclude that they took place in a religious setting. He may go further and conclude that they cannot be explained by either human behavior or physical science. It is Meier's view that the historian then reaches a threshold he or she cannot cross. The historian cannot deny or affirm that Jesus' miraculous actions were done by the power of God. To do either would be "to enter the domain of philosophy or theology." When Crossan concludes that "the religious miracle and the magical effect are in no way substantially distinct,"[7] he has ruled out the reality of Jesus' startling deeds. Meier's challenge would be: Does Crossan do so as a historian or does he do so in the light of his philosophical or theological outlook?

II. MIRACLES AND THE ANCIENT WORLD

Ultimately, the key to learning about the past is to enter the past. When we return to the time of Jesus and outlook of his world, we do find some skepticism about miracles, but this view is confined largely to the educated elite, particularly to philosophers. As Meier puts it: "On the whole, however, the ancient Greco-Roman world was one in which miracles were accepted as part of the religious landscape."[8] With little or no knowledge of what actually caused things to happen, ancient peoples attributed events to supernatural intervention. In a sense everything was miraculous; some occurrences were just more so.

An example can be seen in the medical treatment carried out in the ancient world. Doctors at the time attempted to ameliorate various illnesses. Some of their methods were fairly sophisticated and effective. However, such procedures were accompanied by petitions for a cure made to a god or the gods. What we would call hospitals today were, in those days, religious shrines. At the beginning of the common era it was the Greco-Roman god Aesculapius who was most frequently so petitioned.

The search for the Jesus of history must take into account these differences in outlook. As Meier notes:

> A major problem that faces the modern historian seeking to enter into the thought world of the first century A.D. is not the objections to miracles by the elite but the all-too-ready acceptance of them by ordinary people. Naturally, this has ramifications for any attempt to judge the historicity of the miracle stories in the Gospels.[9]

Even with such a handicap the gospels do tell us much of the role of the "startling deeds" attributed to Jesus during his public life.

III. DEEDS OF POWER AND
THE LANGUAGE OF THE BIBLE

The Bible, in either Hebrew or Greek, has no exact equivalent for the word *miracle*. In the New Testament the Greek word often translated as "miracle" is *dynamis,* but not consistently. Thus, in the *New American Bible* we have Jesus saying, "When that day comes, many will plead with me, 'Lord, Lord,...did we not do many miracles in your name as well?'" (Mt 7:22). By contrast, the same verse in the *New Revised Standard Version* reads: "On that day many will say to me, 'Lord, Lord, did we not…do many deeds of power in your name?'" Given the complexities in determining the meaning of *miracle,* one concludes that "deeds of power" is the better translation.

The Hebrew Bible and the gospels both reflect the view of the ancient world when it comes to reporting "miracles." John L. McKenzie observes that, "although it was written after the birth of [Greek] philosophical and scientific speculation, [the New Testament] shows little or no conception of nature as a systematic unity governed by fixed principles and laws of causality."[10] Thus the definition of *miracle* as "an event that appears unexplainable by the laws of nature" does not reflect the thought-world of the biblical authors. Nor would it define what Josephus meant when he spoke of Jesus' "startling deeds."

Such deeds were not regarded as necessarily rare in the ancient world. The attitude of the Jews was "that from the time of the prophet Elijah, Jews believed that holy men were able to exert their will on natural phenomena."[11] The Gentiles were no less expectant of "startling deeds" from those who were in power.

The Roman historian Suetonius wrote that in 69 C.E. the following took place:

> Vespasian, still rather bewildered in his new role of Emperor, felt a certain lack of authority and impressiveness; yet both these attributes were granted him. As he sat on the Tribunal, two laborers, one blind, the other lame, approached him together, begging to be healed. Apparently the god Serapis had promised them in a dream that if Vespasian would consent to spit in the blind man's eyes, and touch the lame man's leg with his heel, both would be made well….The charm worked.[12]

It will hardly escape our notice that Jesus is shown to have performed deeds of power similar to those attributed to Vespasian, for example, healing the blind man (Mk 8:23; Jn 9:6).

IV. JESUS AND DEEDS OF POWER

A. The Synoptic Accounts

It is hard to imagine that Jesus performed "deeds of power" during his years in Nazareth. Were it so, why would his family and his fellow

Nazoreans be startled by his later conduct? Especially when we see how pervasive such activity was in the accounts of the evangelists. The Marcan version is typical:

> Certainly the most striking characteristic about Mark's Jesus is his ability to do remarkable deeds. Of the four hundred and twenty-five verses that make up the first ten chapters of the first gospel, two hundred are devoted to the wondrous exploits of Jesus. They begin with his "debut" in the synagogue of Capernaum when he exorcises an unclean spirit. They end on the outskirts of Jericho where Jesus restores the sight of Bartimaeus. In fact, one or more wondrous deeds occur in each of these first chapters.
>
> The variety of the deeds is no less impressive. During Jesus' public life he is seen curing a fever, leprosy, paralysis, a withered hand, internal bleeding, a deaf mute, blindness. On one occasion, it would appear that Jesus brought a child back to life. He also performed exorcisms, the driving out evil spirits.[13]

In addition to these individual incidents, Mark recounts that in Capernaum the "whole city was gathered around the door [where Jesus was staying]. And he cured many who were sick with various diseases, and cast out many demons." Wherever Jesus appeared, "all who had diseases pressed upon him to touch him" (1:33–34; 3:10). When he was recognized all the people "rushed about that whole region and began to bring the sick on mats to wherever they heard he was. And wherever [Jesus] went, into villages or cities or farms, they laid the sick in the marketplaces, and begged him that they might touch even the fringe of his cloak; and all who touched it were healed" (6:55–56). Jesus also calmed storms at sea, walked on the sea and on two occasions fed a large number of people on small amounts of food.[14]

These wondrous acts of Jesus form an integral and essential part of Mark's gospel. Any attempt at expurgation of the miraculous renders the document unintelligible. The same is true for Matthew and Luke, who present a similar picture, even adding to the number of wondrous deeds.

B. The Gospel of John

What we have been speaking of as "deeds of power" are referred to in the Fourth Gospel as "signs," *semionis* in the Greek. For example, when Jesus has changed water into wine, we have the following: "Jesus did this, the first of his signs, in Cana of Galilee, and revealed his glory; and his disciples believed in him" (2:11). Later, when Jesus has cured the son of a royal official, we are told: "Now this was the second sign that Jesus did after coming from Judea to Galilee" (4:46, 54). The reader is drawn to look beyond the deed of power itself to a deeper meaning. "[The miracles] are signs of the reality of Jesus as the Son of God and saviour of mankind, of the manifest intervention of God in the world of Jesus."[15]

John presents us with very vivid descriptions of several of Jesus' signs. We have already mentioned the changing of water into wine and the curing of the royal official's son. There is also curing of the cripple at the pool of Bethesda, multiplying loaves and fishes, restoring sight to a blind man and, the climatic sign, raising of Lazarus.[16] Each of these events highlighted an aspect of Jesus' message. The creation of an abundance of food and drink spoke to the glory of the age to come. Cures of illnesses, crippling and blindness spoke to the freedom promised. The raising of a dead man held out the promise of a resurrection. In John's gospel Jesus' deeds of power go beyond being the simply startling to become symbols of a hidden reality.

C. Attesting to the Authority of Jesus

An important, perhaps crucial, result of Jesus' deeds of power is seen when Jesus makes his debut in Capernaum's synagogue. Jesus has cured a man possessed, and we see the reaction of the onlookers: "They were all amazed, and they kept on asking one another, 'What is this? A new teaching—with authority!'" (Mk 1:27). Later, in another synagogue, Jesus astounds his hearers and they say: "Where did this man get all this? What is this wisdom that has been given to him? What deeds of power are being done by his hands!" (Mk 6:2). It is interesting to note here that the deeds of power served for Jesus the same purpose they served for Emperor Vespasian. They reinforced his claim to authority, a political claim in the emperor's case, a religious claim in Jesus' case.

Yet deeds of power, as such, were not unambiguous affirmations. They could be given a sinister implication. We see this when "the scribes who came down from Jerusalem said, 'He [Jesus] has Beelzebul, and by the ruler of the demons he casts out demons'" (Mk 3:22). In a world that did not question the existence of evil supernatural powers, startling deeds could have other than benign implications. Apparently Jesus' opponents could and did question the origin of his powers. Jesus is directly asked: "By what authority are you doing these things? Who gave you this authority to do them?" (Mk 11:28). Obviously there were those who saw Jesus work wonders and yet refused to accept his authority.

D. The Role of Faith

Since deeds of power did not compel acceptance of Jesus' authority, we find in them another dimension. On most occasions Jesus' deeds of power are done simply when Jesus himself perceives a need or responds to a request. Significantly, though, in a number of instances an additional factor is present. We have the following vivid scene in Mark:

> Now there was a woman who had been suffering from hemorrhages for twelve years. She had endured much under many physicians, and had spent all that she had; and she was no better, but rather grew worse. She had heard about Jesus, and came up behind him in the crowd and touched his cloak, for she said, "If I but touch his clothes, I will be made well." Immediately her hemorrhage stopped; and she felt in her body that she was healed of her disease. Immediately aware that power had gone forth from him, Jesus turned about in the crowd and said, "Who touched my clothes?" And his disciples said to him, "You see the crowd pressing in on you; how can you say, 'Who touched me?'" He looked all around to see who had done it. But the woman, knowing what had happened to her, came in fear and trembling, fell down before him, and told him the whole truth. He said to her, "Daughter, your faith has made you well; go in peace, and be healed of your disease." (5:25–34)

In attributing a number of deeds of power to Jesus, Mark frequently cites the role of faith,[17] as we see again when Jesus passes through Jericho on his way up to Jerusalem. A blind man pleads for the restoration of his sight: "Jesus said to him, 'Go; your faith has made you well.' Immediately he regained his sight" (10:52). There is a sense that trusting in Jesus somehow draws power from him.

Nor need the faith be on the part of the one acted on by Jesus' deed of power. At one point several men attempt to bring a paralyzed man to

Jesus. Barred by the crowd, they break a hole in the roof and lower the unfortunate one down. It is on seeing the faith of these men that Jesus is moved to cure the victim of paralysis (2:3–5).

Later, we have this event in Mark: "Then one of the leaders of the synagogue named Jairus came and, when he saw him, fell at his feet and begged him repeatedly, 'My little daughter is at the point of death. Come and lay your hands on her, so that she may be made well, and live.'" Jesus proceeds to the house of Jairus, but while they are on the way the news arrives that the girl is dead. "But overhearing what they said, Jesus said to the leader of the synagogue, 'Do not fear, only believe.'" The reward of the leader's faith is the restoration of the child to life (5:22–42).

Mark presents the same sequence when Jesus encounters a man whose son is suffering from what we now know to be epilepsy. The man begs Jesus to cure his son, to which Jesus replies: "All things can be done for the one who believes." The man then cries out, "I believe; help my unbelief!" (9:17ff.) Again, it is trust that somehow calls forth the deed of power.

If faith draws deeds of power from Jesus, its lack has the opposite effect. When Jesus meets with skepticism in Nazareth, Mark tells the reader: "And he could do no deed of power there, except that he laid his hands on a few sick people and cured them. And he was amazed at their unbelief" (6:5–6).

The role of faith is not confined to Mark. In Matthew we have the cure of the centurion's slave, where Jesus remarks: "Truly I tell you, in no one in Israel have I found such faith....Go; let it be done for you according to your faith" (8:10–13; see also Lk 7:2–10). It is also interesting that to Mark's story of the Syrophoenician woman who asked for her daughter's cure (7:26–30), Matthew adds, "Woman, great is your faith! Let it be done for you as you wish" (15:28).

The evangelists are certainly reassuring their readers that trust in Jesus will prove effective. Nevertheless, their emphasis on the role of faith may reveal a feature of the actual ministry of Jesus. He may have been what is known as a faith healer, one whose powers were somehow evoked by belief in the healer. It is easy to disparage some modern practitioners of such healing, but in the ancient world deeds of power, particularly cures, involved religious faith. If he was seen as a Hasid, Jesus' faith healing would not have been unexpected.

E. Exorcisms

At the time of Jesus belief in the existence of demonic powers characterized the views of both Jews and Gentiles. We can see this outlook in such early Christian writers as Paul: "I imply that what pagans sacrifice, they sacrifice to demons and not to God. I do not want you to be partners with demons" (1 Cor 10:20). In another letter attributed to the Apostle, we also find, "For our struggle is not against enemies of blood and flesh, but against the rulers, against the authorities, against the cosmic powers of this present darkness, against the spiritual forces of evil in the heavenly places" (Eph 6:12). Similarly: "Now the Spirit expressly says that in later times some will renounce the faith by paying attention to deceitful spirits and teachings of demons" (1 Tm 4:1). In another New Testament writing we read, "Even the demons believe—and shudder" (Jas 2:19). Again: "These are demonic spirits, performing signs" (Rv 16:14). Along with this outlook went the conviction that such demons could "possess" a person as well as be the cause of diseases. Thus it is not easy to distinguish between exorcisms and cures.

In the light of such an outlook we are not surprised that among Jesus' deeds of power were exorcisms. In Mark, Jesus is confronted with a particularly vivid example of possession:

> They came to the other side of the sea, to the country of the Gerasenes. And when [Jesus] had stepped out of the boat, immediately a man out of the tombs with an unclean spirit met him. He lived among the tombs; and no one could restrain him any more, even with a chain; for he had often been restrained with shackles and chains, but the chains he wrenched apart, and the shackles he broke in pieces; and no one had the strength to subdue him. Night and day among the tombs and on the mountains he was always howling and bruising himself with stones. (5:1–5)

Jesus frees the man of what appears to have been a number of demons.[18]

As Jesus traveled about, exorcisms were apparently part of his routine: "And he went throughout Galilee, proclaiming the message in their synagogues and casting out demons" (Mk 1:39). On other occasions, as with the Gerasene demoniac, Jesus' deeds of power are specifically exorcisms

(Mk 1:23–26; 7:26–30). In some instances a cure and an exorcism are combined as with the epileptic boy who is cured by the driving out of an evil spirit (Mk 9:17–27). This confirms what we saw above, that disease and possession were not rigidly distinct.

The symbolic element, exorcism, should also be taken into account. There is frequent reference in early Christian writings to the "evil one." Matthew uses similar language, as does John.[19] In exorcising evil spirits Jesus is showing his power over evil and is foreshadowing his eventual defeat of the "evil one." Later we see how such an expectation reflects Jesus' vision of what is to come.

Chapter Seven

THE TITLES OF JESUS

I. THE PROPHET

An insight into a historic figure can be gained from the manner in which others spoke of him. We have tried to picture the Jesus of history as a Hasid, but we do not have any record of Jesus being so designated. True, Josephus referred to Jesus as "a wise man...a doer of startling deeds, a teacher," but did he mean an Hasid, specifically? We cannot know. Yet we do have other titles accorded to Jesus in the New Testament.

Vermes states, "No expert would deny that the gospels portray Jesus as wearing the mantle of a prophet."[1] Indeed, the widest possible range of people refers to Jesus as a prophet. The disciples of Jesus note that he is called such (Mk 8:28). The crowds are said to so identify Jesus (Mt 21:11, 46). Those in the entourage of Herod say the same (Mk 6:15). Even Jesus' enemies give him the title! Finally, though indirectly, Jesus refers to himself as a prophet (Mt 13:57; Lk 13:33), although Vermes cautions, "Doubtless, it would be an exaggeration to claim that Jesus positively proclaimed himself to be a prophet."[2]

The roots of the Hebrew prophet *(nabi)* lie deep in the culture of the ancient Near East. There seem to have been groups regarded as "prophets" who roamed the countryside (cf. 1 Sm 10:5). Still, "[Hebrew] prophetism is generally recognized by scholars as a uniquely distinctive [Hebrew] phenomena."[3] The classical Hebrew prophet appears along with the monarchy in the tenth century B.C.E. and ends following the Babylonian Exile in the sixth century B.C.E. with the prophet Joel. From a reference in 1 Maccabees it would appear that the Jewish priesthood guided the leadership as was once the role of the prophet. "The Jews and their priests have resolved that Simon should be their leader and high priest forever, until a trustworthy prophet should arise" (1 Mc 14:41).

As we make the transition to the common era, another hope arises: "The expectation was prevalent in inter-Testamental Judaism of a heavenly messenger who, at the end of time, would deliver God's final words to Israel."[4] One possible candidate for this role was a returned Elijah. The prophet Malachi had predicted: "Lo, I will send you the prophet Elijah before the great and terrible day of the LORD comes (4:5). There apparently were those who thought Jesus was such a figure (Mk 6:15; 8:28). However, later the reference was attached John the Baptizer rather than Jesus (Mt 17:10–12).

There is another visualization of the expected eschatological prophet that relates to Moses:

> The LORD your God will raise up for you a prophet like me from among your own people; you shall heed such a prophet....I will raise up for them a prophet like you from among their own people; I will put my words in the mouth of the prophet, who shall speak to them everything that I command. (Dt 18:15, 18)

In the Acts of the Apostles this passage is applied to Jesus (3:22–26).

Even though references to Jesus as a prophet are found in John (6:14; 7:40), the title as applied to Jesus fades. As Vermes points out: "That the title, after a promising beginning, made no further headway, seems to have been due to the coincidence, unfortunate or not, that during the formation of primitive Christian thought, there was a plethora in Palestine of pseudo-prophets."[5] Yet, among the Jews who associated with him and those who heard and saw him, there were certainly those who saw him as the hoped-for eschatological prophet. Indeed, there is reason to believe that Jesus himself preferred such a designation, as we read in Vermes.[6] It is not beyond the realm of possibility that one regarded as a Hasid would be thought to also wear the mantle of a prophet.

II. THE LORD

"'Lord' is a New Testament key word."[7] Indeed, it is used twice as frequently as "Christ" and appears in Christian scripture with the frequency of Jesus' own name. Some believe this to be a clear indication that Jesus was called "lord" in his own time and by his earliest followers. Others emphatically disagree, attributing the use of the title to the period when Christianity fell under the influence of Hellenism. The nexus of the disagreement is that *Lord* (*Adonai* in Hebrew and *Kyrios* in Greek) is used as a title for the Deity and thus its use could indicate a belief in Jesus' divinity. It is generally agreed that the full realization of Jesus' Divine nature developed over an extended period of time.

However, it is still possible that Jesus was referred to as lord in his lifetime. "Thus in Jewish Aramaic the designation '(the) lord,' is appropriate in connection with God, or a secular dignitary, or an authoritative teacher, or a person renowned for his spiritual or supernatural force."[8] In this latter usage it could have been a title accorded a Hasid such as Jesus.

III. THE SON OF GOD

In the authentic letters of Paul—Galatians, 1 Corinthians and Romans—Jesus is spoken of as "the Son of God" in terms that express, at the least, a special relationship between him and the Deity.[9] It is hardly surprising, then, to find in the gospels that this title is applied to Jesus by any number of individuals, including God himself: "And a voice came from heaven, 'You are my Son, the Beloved; with you I am well pleased'" (Mk 1:11). Finally, when asked directly by his accusers, "Are you…the Son of the Blessed One?" Jesus replied, "I am" (Mk 14:61–62).

We return to our general question: In what sense might the title "son of God" been applied to the Jesus of history and in what sense might Jesus have accepted it? In the light of the strict monotheism of Judaism at the time, it is hard to imagine how Jesus would have accorded divinity to himself or how any other Jew would have done so. But need the title necessarily denote divinity?

The Hebrew Bible speaks of the Jews as the "sons [children] of God." We read in Exodus, "Thus says the LORD: Israel is my firstborn son" (4:22).[10] King David is spoken of as God's son is a special sense when the Lord says: "I will be a father to him, and he shall be a son to me" (2 Sm 7:14). This same relationship is seen to apply to David's successors (Pss 2:7; 89:26–27). The language obviously does not imply that such "sons" are divine.

More to our concern is the application in inter-testamental times of the title "son of God" to the just and saintly man, in particular the Hasid. Vermes argues that

> part of the Synoptic evidence concerning the divine sonship of Jesus corresponds exactly of the Galilean miracle-working Hasid....There is, in other words, no reason to contest the possibility, and even the great probability, that already during his life Jesus was spoken of and addressed by admiring believers as *son of God*.[11]

But would Jesus have thought of himself as a son of God had that title no implication of divinity? In discussing Jesus as a man of prayer, we noted that Jesus addressed God in an intimate way as *Abba*, a characteristic he shared with the Hasidim. Again Vermes notes: "One of the distinguishing features of ancient Hasidic piety is its habit of alluding to God precisely as 'Father.'"[12] The implication is that Jesus as a Hasid might have regarded himself as the son of God in the same sense.

IV. THE SON OF MAN

The phrase "the son of man" appears seventy-eight times in the gospels but only three times elsewhere (Acts 7:56; Rv 1:13; 14:14). The most widely debated and confusing title (or designation) applied to Jesus is Son of Man (in Aramaic, *bar 'e nasa'*). The questions whether the historical Jesus used the title and, if so, in what sense he used it have received every answer imaginable.[13]

Jesus is shown as customarily using the phrase to speak of himself; yet no one, friend or enemy, queries its meaning or objects to its use. Again the question: Did the Jesus of history use the phrase and, if so, what did he mean by it?

The simplest answer lies in the fact that *bar 'e nasa'* can be an Aramaic circumlocution for speaking of the "human" or for referring to oneself. Mark gives us two possible examples of the former usage (2:10, 28). And when Jesus speaks of the impending fate of the "son of man" (8:38; 9:9, 12, 31) he would have been making a thinly veiled reference to himself. His hearers, aware of the idiom, would have taken no notice of it.

Later, the early followers of Jesus, recalling his use of the phrase, would have connected it with the words of Daniel:

> I saw one like a human being
> coming with the clouds of heaven. (Dn 7:13)[14]

Making this connection would give rise to apocalyptic expressions such as "then they will see 'the Son of Man coming in clouds' with great power and glory" (Mk 13:26). This is also the case in Jesus' climactic response to the high priest: "You will see the Son of Man seated at the right hand of the Power,' and 'coming with the clouds of heaven'" (Mk 14:62). "There is, in addition," Vermes concludes, "no valid argument to prove that any of the gospel passages directly or indirectly referring to Daniel 7:13 may be traced back to Jesus."[15]

Raymond Brown, agreeing with much of what Vermes concludes, nevertheless holds out the possibility that Jesus himself could have laid the foundation for the later attribution of the "son of man" phrase. Brown reasons that faced with a hostile reaction to his mission, Jesus saw in the figure from Daniel a promise of his own ultimate vindication. According to Brown, "there is reason to believe that in [Mark] 14:62 we may be close to the mindset and style of Jesus himself."[16]

V. THE CHRIST

The roots of the title *messiah* in Jewish tradition reach back to David, the anointed ruler of Israel (1 Sm 16:13). When we come to the common era, Vermes concludes: "If in the inter-Testamental era a man claimed, or was proclaimed, to be 'the Messiah,' his listeners would as a matter of course have assumed that he was referring to the Davidic Redeemer."[17] At the same time, Vermes points out, "a wide range of Messianic ideas and images arose in the various religious-social circles of Palestinian Jewry."[18] Thus, beyond the Davidic element, we are not able to determine precisely what a contemporary of Jesus would have meant by the messianic title.[19]

When we come to the early Christian communities, few if any would dispute the conclusion that "'the Christ'…belonged to the heart and kernel of the earliest phase of Christian belief."[20] We find the common expression "Jesus Christ" in the opening line of the earliest Christian document, 1 Thessalonians, and within a generation of Jesus' death his followers are known as Christians. The core conviction that Jesus was the Messiah certainly played a role in the presentation of Jesus in the gospels. But, again, we are confronted with questions: Did Jesus himself lay claim to the title? Was Jesus ever addressed by the title in his lifetime?

Regarding the first question, there is a general agreement among scholars, including Vermes and Brown, that Jesus never used the title of Messiah to describe himself. However, as Brown, affirms, " I judge it plausible that during Jesus' lifetime some of his followers thought him to be the Messiah.…Jesus, confronted with this identification, responded ambivalently."[21] It could also be that others, those who wished to destroy Jesus, tried to present him as making messianic claims in order to reinforce their accusations of attempted sedition. In fact, given the effectiveness of the charge, it is understandable that Jesus, no matter what his self-awareness of his role, would have been cautious in making any reference to messianism.

What is puzzling is how a title with such a strong Jewish background gained such currency as Christianity became increasingly Gentile. There is a possible explanation. The earliest Christians were Jews who were distinguished from their fellow Jews by their acceptance of Jesus as the Messiah, something their co-religionists rejected. These followers of the Nazorean were then called "Messianists" by their Jewish opponents. The Greek form of appellation, "Christian," stuck. As Vermes observes: "In short, the success of the Messianic idea probably owed more to polemical convenience than to theological usefulness."[22]

VI. SELF-AWARENESS

Prophet, Lord, Son of God, Son of Man and *Christ,* all may indicate ways people made reference to the Jesus of history, some at different stages of his ministry. As we have seen, it is never absolutely clear in what manner, if any, Jesus accepted or understood these titles. Perhaps the best we can say is that these titles were "in the air" and that some, directly or indirectly, became part of Jesus' own self-awareness.

There remains a specific challenge, however, for those believers who hold that Jesus was by nature divine. We have already noted the difficulty of imagining how a pious Jew whose religion would brook no notion of a human being sharing divinity could have understood even a hint that he himself was divine. Moreover, his Jewish contemporaries and his earliest followers, also Jewish, would have had the same difficulty.[23]

The New Testament itself displays considerable ambiguity on this very point. Paul, writing to Rome, says of Jesus that he "was declared to be Son of God with power according to the spirit of holiness by resurrection from the dead" (1:4). The implication is that Jesus was not "son of God" during his lifetime.[24] Mark, in turn, indicates that Jesus is himself informed of his divinity at his baptism by John: "And a voice came from heaven, 'You are my Son, the Beloved; with you I am well pleased'" (1:11). From the context it would appear that the voice was for the benefit of Jesus himself. Moreover, Mark presents us with a Jesus who displays significant human limitations.

In Matthew and Luke, Jesus' parents are shown to be aware of his divine origins. Further, in Luke, the youthful Jesus himself knows this as well. Discovered in the great Temple he tells his parents: "Why were you searching for me? Did you not know that I must be in my Father's house?" (2:49). In the Fourth Gospel, Jesus is eternally divine as the Word: "In the beginning was the Word, and the Word was with God, and the Word was God....And the Word became flesh and lived among us, and we have seen his glory, the glory as of a father's only son, full of grace and truth" (1:1, 14). In John's gospel Jesus is fully aware of his divinity.

As the centuries passed the Christian communities faced an increasing dilemma. On the one hand were those who thought that in order to preserve the belief that Jesus was divine it was necessary to see him as less than fully human. Others, defending Jesus' complete humanity, saw him as less than fully divine. The result was a bitter, divisive conflict, resolved only in the fourth and fifth centuries C.E. with the promulgation of the teaching on the Holy Trinity by the first of the church ecumenical councils.

Still today, for the believer in Jesus' divinity, there remains a challenge. Being human is something we experience. If the Jesus of history, due to his divinity, did not share that experience then there is a profound sense in which he was not one of us. Indeed, this can often be seen in our depictions of Jesus. He can so "glow" with divinity that he seems unreal. We cannot believe he experienced the world as we do. The New Testament document known as the letter to Hebrews challenges just such a view: "For we do not have a high priest [Jesus] who is unable to sympathize with our weaknesses, but we have one who in every respect has been tested as we are, yet without sin" (4:15). This would hardly be true if Jesus' divinity suppressed any and all of his human experiences.

Still, there are those who believe that their faith in Jesus' divinity is threatened when he is depicted with *any* human limitation. I believe this explains the sometimes fierce reaction to films portraying a very human Jesus, such as Pier Pasolini's *The Gospel According to Matthew* and Martin Scorsese's *The Last Temptation of Christ*. There might well have been a similar reaction to Mark's presentation of a Jesus with very human limitations![25] The subsequent gospels appear to reflect just such a response. Yet Mark himself may have been challenging his own community's proneness to see Jesus as a divine being masquerading in human form.[26]

Determining who Jesus of Nazareth was challenged Jesus' contemporaries as well as his earliest followers. Perhaps it challenged Jesus himself. The titles applied to him are evidence of various attempts to meet this challenge. To some degree they both reveal and conceal his identity. Yet, it is true also that outstanding historical figures, even the most recent, transcend our understanding of them. This is no less true of the Jesus of history.

Chapter Eight

JESUS AND THE KINGDOM OF GOD

I. A DIVISION IN JESUS' MINISTRY

The reader is certainly aware of the controversy over which of the sayings in the gospels can be regarded as authentically those of Jesus. Meier observes: "The time frame and plot line of each evangelist are his own creation."[1] He concludes that "between Jesus' baptism and the last week of [Jesus'] life, there is no before or after."[2] To establish a sequence of Jesus' sayings and the events of his public ministry cannot be done readily. Still, the proposition that there was a shift in emphasis as Jesus' ministry progressed is not entirely without support.

We have posited that Jesus appeared to his contemporaries as a wonder-working Hasid, moving through the villages of lower Galilee and adjacent areas. Such a figure would have dispensed sage advice and enlivened his teaching with apt stories. He called his hearers to a life of Jewish piety that reflected the rural life that Jesus himself experienced. We have seen how that message, especially when backed up by "marvelous deeds," would have given rise to the opposition of the urban Pharisees. Still, they and others do seem to have overreacted—unless there is another element.

We needn't posit an abrupt change in Jesus' message. There would have continued to be a Hasidic dimension to his teaching. Nor can we with any precision determine the point at which something new appeared. Even riskier would be to hazard an opinion as to the reason for the shift in emphasis. Nevertheless, I do propose that such a change did take place and that it was to have the gravest of consequences.

II. JESUS, HERALD OF THE KINGDOM

That new element is reflected in the phrase "kingdom of God." As Vermes notes: "From the mere frequency of the phases, 'Kingdom of God' and 'Kingdom of Heaven'—they figure no less than a hundred times in the Synoptic Gospels—it is reasonable to infer that the concepts which they reflect played a important part in the teaching of Jesus."[3] It is not only the frequency of the phrase's use that attests to the centrality of the theme, but the variety of contexts in which "kingdom of God" is found. "At the very least, 'kingdom of God' was a major component of Jesus' message."[4] There is the possibility that the phrase only gradually emerged as such a component.

Moreover, the criterion of discontinuity can be used here as testimony to the authenticity of the phrase as attributed to Jesus. It is largely absent from the Jewish sources: "The precise phrase 'kingdom of God' does not occur as such in the Hebrew OT and occurrences in the deuterocanonical/apocryphal books of the OT, the OT pseudepigrapha, Qumran, Philo, Josephus and most of the targums are either rare or nonexistent."[5]

In the New Testament references to the kingdom of God are similarly rare. Outside the gospels the phrase appears fewer than twenty times. The implication is that "the frequent appearances of 'kingdom of God' on the lips of the Synoptic Jesus cannot be traced to its popularity and regular use in either pre-Christian Judaism or first-century Christianity."[6] It is clear, then, that Jesus' use of the "kingdom of God" phrase was not something he shared with the Hasidim. All of this indicates that the New Testament use of "kingdom of God" is a tradition going back to the Jesus of history.

However, in affirming that usage we must not overlook this reminder from Meier that, "whatever his own message, Jesus was working within a religious tradition and with a set of religious symbols that had their own long history. If Jesus wished to reshape those symbols to fit his own message he had to do so within the constraints of history."[7] We are brought back to what was observed earlier—that Jesus was a Jew, well-versed in the riches of that religious milieu. It was out of that background that Jesus shaped his message.

III. THE KINGDOM OF GOD IN THE JEWISH TRADITIONS

A. *The Jewish Scriptures*

The Hebrew phrase for "kingdom of God," *malkût yahweh,* is not found in the Hebrew canon. Nevertheless, references to God as a king are found, and such regal references to God underwent a development over the centuries. Actually, regarding a god as a king extends back to the ancient cultures of the Middle East. The Israelites appear to have adopted such a custom early on as we see in Exodus: "The LORD will reign forever and ever" (15:18). We have similar language in Psalms:

The LORD has established his throne in the heavens,
  and his kingdom rules over all. (103:19)[8]

Later there appears a reluctance among the Jews to designate a person as their temporal ruler. Around the tenth century B.C.E., when the Israelites adopted a more centralized governance, first under Saul and then under David, the transition appears to have caused some tension. We read in I Samuel: "The LORD said to Samuel, 'Listen to the voice of the people in all that they say to you; for they have not rejected you, but they have rejected me from being king over them'" (8:7). The Davidic monarchy then established survived until after the Exile, disappearing in the late sixth century B.C.E.

However, the vision of God as king was not lost. It is reflected in First Isaiah:[9] "I saw the Lord sitting on a throne, high and lofty; and the hem of his robe filled the temple....My eyes have seen the King, the LORD of hosts!" (6:1, 5). Later, with Second Isaiah, the identification is specific: "I am the LORD, your Holy One, the Creator of Israel, your King" (43:15).[10] Similar language is found in Jeremiah.[11]

B. *The Inter-Testamental Period*

As we approach the inter-testamental period we increasingly see an expectation for the future. In Zechariah we read: "And the LORD will become king over all the earth; on that day the LORD will be one and his name one" (14:9). The Book of Daniel has a similar outlook:

I blessed the Most High,
  and praised and honored the one who lives forever.

For his sovereignty is an everlasting sovereignty,
> and his kingdom endures from generation to generation. (4:34; also
> 2:44)

In our discussion of the title son of man we spoke of its source in
Daniel. More is said there of that enigmatic figure:

As I watched in the night visions,
> I saw one like a human being [son of man]
>> coming with the clouds of heaven.
> And he came to the Ancient One
>> and was presented before him.
To him was given dominion
> and glory and kingship,
that all peoples, nations, and languages
> should serve him.
His dominion is an everlasting dominion
> that shall not pass away,
and his kingship is one
> that shall never be destroyed. (7:13–14)

One wonders if it is here that we have the crucial link. Jesus made use
of a phrase that had a regal reference.

C. Summary

This very brief survey of the Jewish traditions concerning their
God's regal role shows the richness and complexity of that legacy. As
Meier observes: "The OT supplied Jesus with the language, symbols,
and story of God's kingly rule, and hence with a range of meanings.
What he fashioned out of that heritage only an investigation of his sayings and actions will show."[12] At some point Jesus, drawing on his Jewish heritage, turned his attention to the prospect of "God's kingly rule"
and its implications.

As Meier states:

> Still, it is conceivable that Jesus, as a creative thinker and teacher, con-
> sciously reworked what was largely an eschatological symbol to signify
> either God's timeless, ever-present reign or its present, definitive real-
> ization in Jesus' words and deeds.[13]

Continuing, Meier makes a crucial point: "It would have been necessary for Jesus to make an important shift in the symbol's significance clear to his audience if he did not want to guarantee that he would be misunderstood."[14]

Actually, as we will see, Jesus described the kingdom of God in two ways. In one aspect God's rule over the universe is something to be revealed in the future. In another aspect the kingdom is something already present. These views are not contradictory but supplementary, two dimensions of the same reality.

III. THE FUTURE KINGDOM

A. The Our Father

There is an ancient Aramaic prayer known as the *Qaddish*. The following are relevant excerpts:

> Magnified and sanctified be his great name...
> May he establish his kingdom during your life...
> May the prayers and supplication of all Israel be acceptable before their
> Father who is in heaven...[15]

Precise dating of the *Qaddish* is not possible, but certainly it had roots going back to the lifetime of Jesus. His own version expresses much the same hope:

> "Pray then in this way:
> Our Father in heaven,
>   hallowed be your name.
>   Your kingdom come." (Mt 6:9–10; Lk 11:2)

> In short, when Jesus prays that God's kingdom come, he is simply expressing in a more abstract phrase the eschatological hope of the later part of the OT and the pseudepigrapha that God would come on the last day to save and restore his people Israel.[16]

We tend to think of the Our Father as a Christian prayer. From the lips of Jesus himself, however, it was the plea of a pious Israelite for Yahweh to come and establish God's eternal kingdom.

B. *The Last Supper*

Later we will treat in detail the final meal Jesus shared with this disciples. However, for now we note that at the beginning of the meal Mark has Jesus saying: "Truly I tell you, I will never again drink of the fruit of the vine until that day when I drink it new in the kingdom of God" (14:25; also Lk 22:18). It is a time when Jesus is aware that his mission is approaching its end. The passage reflects a tradition that he expected that the kingdom was shortly to come.

An abundance of wine was used to characterize God's coming to save his people:

In that day the mountains shall drip sweet wine. (Jl 3:18)
I will restore the fortunes of my people Israel,
    and they shall rebuild the ruined cities and inhabit them;
they shall plant vineyards and drink their wine,
    and they shall make gardens and eat their fruit. (Am 9:14)
Then the people of Ephraim shall become like warriors,
    and their hearts shall be glad as with wine. (Zec 10:7)

In intending to abstain temporarily from wine, Jesus appears to project the coming of that kingdom into the near future.

C. *The Eschatological Banquet*

In Matthew we have Jesus saying: "I tell you, many will come from east and west and will eat with Abraham and Isaac and Jacob in the kingdom of heaven, while the heirs of the kingdom will be thrown into the outer darkness" (8:11–12). If we understand that Jesus expected the Gentiles to be joining the eschatological banquet, then he is voicing the earlier hope of the prophet Isaiah:

In days to come
    the mountain of the LORD's house
shall be established as the highest of the mountains,
    and shall be raised above the hills;
all the nations shall stream to it.
    Many peoples shall come and say,
"Come, let us go up to the mountain of the Lord,
    to the house of the God of Jacob;

that he may teach us his ways
    and that we may walk in his paths." (2:2–3)

But who were "the heirs of the kingdom" that were to be replaced at
the end of time by those who "will come from east and west"? Jesus
would not have seen these as the Israelites in general, as did later Christians who had become alienated from the Jewish community. It is more
likely that Jesus' warning was directed at those of his contemporaries
who had rejected his message.

D. *The Beatitudes* (Mt 5:3–12; Lk 6:20–23)

In a group of verses called the Beatitudes, found in both Matthew
and Luke, we read:

"Blessed are you who are poor,
    for yours is the kingdom of God." (Lk 6:20)

Meier writes:

As a specific form of wisdom teaching, beatitudes…were known in
ancient Egypt, Greece, and Israel.…That Jesus as wisdom teacher and
eschatological prophet, would have used beatitudes at times in his
preaching enjoys antecedent probability.[17]

It is in the kingdom to come that Israel's God will bring the blessings
promised to the poor. Here Jesus is echoing the traditions of his people
as we see in Psalms:

Happy are those whose help is the God of Jacob,
    whose hope is in the LORD their God,…
    who executes justice for the oppressed;
    who gives food to the hungry.

The LORD sets the prisoners free;
    the LORD opens the eyes of the blind.
The LORD lifts up those who are bowed down;
    the LORD loves the righteous.
The LORD watches over the strangers;
    he upholds the orphan and the widow. (146:5, 7–9)

It is understandable that Jesus would have held out hope to the oppressed of his day. Given his own background, he was well-aware of the deprivation and sufferings of those around him. Yet, as Meier points out:

> Jesus was not interested in and did not issue pronouncements about concrete social and political reforms either for the world in general or for Israel in particular. He was not proclaiming the reform of the world; he was proclaiming the end of the world.[18]

This brings us to the question: How soon is the eschatological event to be expected?

E. The Note of Urgency

Generally speaking, the Hebrew prophets spoke of events soon to come rather than those in the distant future. In addition, the Middle Eastern mind-set on the future tended to focus on the short term rather than the long term. The Jesus of history seems to have shared those attitudes. His own radical change in lifestyle from a village artisan to a wandering preacher indicates a sense of urgency. A soon-to-be expected "end of the world" would have motivated Jesus' sudden transformation.

Jesus calls for a similar radical change in those who aspire to be his followers. To one such person Jesus says, "You lack one thing; go, sell what you own, and give the money to the poor,…then come, follow me" (Mk 10:21). In *Q* we have a man requesting to first see to his father burial before joining Jesus' entourage. The reply is curt: "Follow me, and let the dead bury their own dead" (Mt 8:22; Lk 9:60). Luke adds another's request to bid farewell to his family, and Jesus responds, "No one who puts a hand to the plow and looks back is fit for the kingdom of God" (9:62). These passages could be seen as directed only to those wishing to be part of his entourage. Yet, there is evidence Jesus issued a wider warning of imminent calamity.

We saw earlier that the parables give us an insight into Jesus' preaching. C. H. Dodd notes:

> The parables are perhaps the most characteristic element in the teaching of Jesus Christ as recorded in the gospels. They have upon them, taken as a whole, the stamp of a highly individual mind, in spite of the re-handling they have inevitably suffered in the course of transmission.

Their appeal to the imagination fixed them in the memory, and gave them a secure place in the tradition. Certainly there is no part of the gospel record, which has for the reader a clearer ring of authenticity.[19]

Several of Jesus' parables call the audience to take decisive action. In Luke we have the parable of the dishonest steward who acts decisively when he is about to lose his position (16:1–8). The story is all the more striking in that the action he takes is embezzlement. Similarly, in the story of the wicked tenants the miscreants take a decisive, if murderously criminal, action to gain ownership of the vineyard (Mk 12:1–9).

Failure to prepare for what is coming is to court disaster. The rich man who counts on a long future loses everything (Lk 12:16–20). The ten foolish bridesmaids are similarly caught unprepared and are barred from the wedding banquet (Mt 25:1–13). In his version of the parable of the Great Banquet, Matthew adds a figure who is invited to the wedding but being improperly dressed—that is, unprepared—perishes (22:1–13).

To what we have said can be added gospel passages indicating that Jesus expected the kingdom to be established in the near future. We noted above that at the Last Supper Jesus' abstinence from drinking wine was only meant to be temporary. Jesus also warns:

> "Truly I tell you, there are some standing here who will not taste death until they see that the kingdom of God has come with power....Truly I tell you, this generation will not pass away until all these things have taken place." (Mk 9:1; 13:30)

Or:

> "When they persecute you in one town, flee to the next; for truly I tell you, you will not have gone through all the towns of Israel before the Son of Man comes." (Mt 10:23)

Since the event did not occur, Jesus was mistaken, which is a troublesome notion to some. Meier, nevertheless, argues that these passages are not authentic. He believes they represent the views of the early church, which did, in fact, expect the imminent coming of the kingdom (see 1 Thes 4:16–17).[20]

IV. THE KINGDOM OF GOD ALREADY PRESENT

A. *Jesus' Parables*

Though he mainly stressed the coming of a future kingdom of God, Jesus also sees that kingdom as already present. Indeed, he says as much in Luke's gospel: "For, in fact, the kingdom of God is among you" (17:21). As examples we have the parables whose rural ambience testifies to their authenticity: In Mark we have Jesus' description, "The kingdom of God is as if someone would scatter seed on the ground, and would sleep and rise night and day, and the seed would sprout and grow, he does not know how" (4:26–27). In like manner, from a tiny mustard seed a great shrub will grow (Mk 4:30–32). Something is present now that will become fully revealed in the future. This hidden aspect of the kingdom is emphasized in the *Q* source: "The kingdom of heaven is like yeast that a woman took and mixed in with three measures of flour until all of it was leavened" (Mt 13:33; Lk 13:21). Finally, in Matthew we have the kingdom pictured as a treasure hidden in a field and as a fine pearl found by a merchant (13:44–46).

B. *Other References*

After a dialogue with the disciples of John the Baptizer (Mt 11:3–6), Jesus says the following: "Truly I tell you, among those born of women no one has arisen greater than John the Baptist; yet the least in the kingdom of heaven is greater than he" (Mt 11:11). Jesus is not speaking of something yet to occur. John, though the least in the kingdom, is still alive at this point and is already part of the kingdom.

In the synoptics, Jesus is accused of exorcising demons by the power of Satan (Mk 3:23–27; Mt 12:25–30; Lk 11:17–23). The *Q* source introduces into the passage the following: "But if it is by the finger of God that I cast out the demons, then the kingdom of God has come to you" (Lk 11:20; Mt 12:28). Since Jesus is, in fact, drawing his power from God, then the promised kingdom is already present. "Jesus does present his exorcisms as proof that the kingdom of God that he proclaims for the future is in some sense already present."[21]

Though the precise relationship between the kingdom-to-come and the kingdom-now is not clear, we can agree with Meier, who writes, "There is no reason to think that this present kingdom is some separate reality, essentially different from the future kingdom soon to arrive."[22] Granting that the Jesus of history held such views and that he increasingly stressed his message about the kingdom, what else can we say?

V. JESUS THE APOCALYPTIC

My suggestion is that, over time, Jesus became more focused on an impending, ultimate calamity when God would establish his kingdom. Such being true, then Jesus' was reflecting the message of his mentor. As Meier concludes, "It may therefore be more accurate to describe John [the Baptizer] as an eschatological prophet tinged with some apocalyptic motifs."[23] We have in John the element of urgency in the face of impending disaster: "Even now the ax is lying at the root of the trees; every tree therefore that does not bear good fruit is cut down and thrown into the fire" (Mt 3:10).

It is possible that as Jesus' preaching became more eschatological, his use of the phrase "son of man" took on an apocalyptic tone, one influenced by the reference in Daniel. Also there were those who now spoke of Jesus as the expected Messianic figure whose appearance was to usher in the final phase of God's plan for Israel's salvation. Even though Jesus may have specifically denied it (Mk 12:35–37), there were those who might have seen in Jesus the possible restoration of the Davidic monarchy. If so, we have what might be the source of the fatal charge leveled against Jesus, the claim that he was "king of the Jews."

Given the political circumstances, there could hardly have been a more dangerous turn of events. The danger would have become all the greater whenever Jesus appeared in Jerusalem itself. Moreover, to those who regarded Jesus as a threat to the status quo, his appearance as a royal claimant presented them with a means of his destruction. The scene is now set for the final tragedy.

Chapter Nine

THE BEGINNING OF THE END

I. THE CHRONOLOGY

A. *The Synoptics*

All the evangelists agree that the final act in the New Testament presentation of the Jesus of history begins with a fateful journey to Jerusalem. For Mark and the other synoptics, there is but a single such journey, climaxing a year's ministry in lower Galilee and surrounding areas. In addition, the events that follow Jesus' arrival in the capital city are carefully arranged over the period of eight days. That chronology gives evidence of an early device to aid the memory of those transmitting the oral tradition. As we have already noted, we have no way of determining the actual sequence of events. John's gospel, as we will see, differs in its account of the final events in Jesus' life.

The following is the basic schema of Mark: On the first day of the week Jesus came up to Jerusalem from Jericho. He entered the city but left almost immediately for nearby Bethany (10:46; 11:1, 11). He and his companions returned to the city the following day (11:12, 15, 19) and again went back to Bethany in the evening. On the third day of the week the group was once more in the city. On all three of these days they visited the Temple. Apparently, on the fourth day Jesus and his disciples remained in Bethany with his host, identified as "Simon the leper" (14:3). Mark's note that "it was two days before the Passover and the festival of Unleavened Bread" (14:1) relates the sequence of events to the days of the week.[1]

On the next day, Thursday, the eve of Passover, preparations for the celebration began. At sunset—by Jewish reckoning, the following day (Passover) began at sunset—Jesus and his disciples returned to the city for the celebratory meal. At its conclusion they left the city for the Mount of Olives (14:12–26). With minor variations Matthew and Luke follow the same chronology.[2] However, as we have seen, they rearrange and augment the material they received from Mark.

B. *John's Gospel*

For all its differences, the Fourth Gospel also betrays a dependence on Mark's chronology. For instance, six days before the crucial Passover,[3] John has Jesus in Bethany (12:1). On the first day of the week Jesus enters Jerusalem (12:12), not, as in the synoptics, for the first time, but rather for the final of several such visits. On the fifth day, though the event is described differently, Jesus shares a final meal with his disciples (13:1ff.). The crucial variation is that the Last Supper is not the Passover meal. It took place on the previous day. Nevertheless, the resemblance between the two chronologies has led many commentators to believe that Mark and John depend on an earlier tradition they have in common.

Our search for the Jesus of history in the gospel accounts of his final days and even hours is particularly difficult. The arrangement of events, the participants, the sayings attributed to Jesus, all are likely determined by the thematic concerns of the evangelists. The possibility of discovering "history remembered" is limited. Yet, in several places that history is discernible: the arrival of Jesus in the Holy City, the dramatic action of his driving the undesirables from the Temple, the plotting against Jesus by Jewish officialdom, Jesus' final meal with his companions, and his concluding command to recall the evening's event.

II. THE ENTRANCE INTO JERUSALEM

A. *Prophecy Historicized*

The synoptic gospels tell of Jesus' first and only visit to the Holy City (Mk 11:1; Mt 21:1; Lk 19:29). The scene is vivid. Acting on a knowledge of what is to come, Jesus sends two of disciples to obtain a mount. Riding on the animal, Jesus appears to engender something of a procession: "Many people spread their cloaks on the road, and others spread leafy branches that they had cut in the fields" (Mk 11:8). Jesus then enters the city amid shouts:

> Hosanna!
>> Blessed is the one who comes in the name of the Lord!
>> Blessed is the coming kingdom of our ancestor David!
> Hosanna in the highest heaven!" (Mk 11:9–10)

John records a similar scene in connection with Jesus' final appearance in Jerusalem (12:12–15).

In their accounts of the event both Matthew and John cite the passage from the prophet Zechariah:

> Rejoice greatly, O daughter Zion!
>> Shout aloud, O daughter Jerusalem!
> Lo, your king comes to you;
>> triumphant and victorious is he,
> humble and riding on a donkey,
>> on a colt, the foal of a donkey. (Zec 9:9)[4]

All the gospels make reference to Psalm 118: "Blessed is the one who comes in the name of the LORD" (v. 26). In the same psalm we have: "Bind the festal procession with branches, up to the horns of the altar" (v. 27). It would appear that it was from these passages that the tradition created the scene of Jesus' regal, even triumphant, entry into Jerusalem.

B. History Remembered

Yet, could there have also been an element of "history remembered"? A clue is provided by another verse from the prophecy of Zechariah: "Then all who survive of the nations that have come against Jerusalem shall go up year after year to worship the King, the LORD of hosts, and to keep the festival of booths" (14:16). That feast, now known as Sukkoth, "was the most important and the most crowded of the three annual pilgrimages to the sanctuary."[5] It was characteristic of the feast's celebration that "for eight days the Jews carried around thyrus, green branches and palms."[6]

In John's gospel Jesus is said to visit the Holy City five times, each on a pilgrimage feast. One of these was the Jewish festival of Booths (7:2–10). Could this be the "history remembered"? It would be a memory of Jesus, surrounded by his followers, carrying such greenery in joyous procession as they entered Jerusalem. Influenced by the prophecy of Zechariah, the gospel traditions transferred that memory to Jesus' final entrance into the Holy City.

III. THE CLEANSING OF THE TEMPLE

We can see the same process at work in the account of Jesus' cleansing of the Temple.[7] It is quite possible that during one of his several visits to the Temple (the Johannine chronology) Jesus could have made a dramatic gesture protesting the commercialization of the Temple rituals. He might have seen these practices as having become oppressive, especially for the poor. Any such action would have easily triggered the opposition of the Jewish leadership, whose status rested on the Temple (Mk 11:18). When the protest occurred and what its circumstances were we cannot know.[8] Still, here might lie "history remembered."

On the other hand, prophecy has also colored the synoptic accounts. Jesus says: "Is it not written, 'My house shall be called a house of prayer...'? But you have made it a den of robbers'" (Mk 11:17; Mt 21:13; Lk 19:46). The reference is to Jeremiah: "Has this house, which is called by my name, become a den of robbers in your sight?" (7:11). Later in the same passage we have Israel threatened for its faithlessness: "And I will bring to an end the sound of mirth and gladness...in the cities of Judah and in the streets of Jerusalem; for the land shall become a waste" (7:34). By the time of the evangelists, Jerusalem and its Temple were in ruins. Christians saw this as the fulfillment of prophecy, one that Jesus had reiterated.

Mark alone adds a crucial phrase: "Is it not written, 'My house shall be called a house of prayer *for all the nations?*'" The reference is to Isaiah: "And the foreigners...these I will bring to my holy mountain, and make them joyful in my house of prayer;...for my house shall be called a house of prayer *for all peoples*" (56:6–7, my emphasis). Mark's community was overwhelmingly Gentile. By linking Jesus' action in the Temple to the spread of Christianity to "the foreigners" as well as to fate of that Temple, we have a further example of "prophecy historicized."

IV. PLOTS AND BETRAYAL

If Jesus, even while still seen as a Hasid, visited Jerusalem and its Temple, his presence must have heightened the tension among himself, the Pharisees and other Jewish authorities. The confrontations recorded in the gospels quite possibly sprang from such encounters. As his ministry progressed, Jesus took a more apocalyptic bent, speaking of the coming of the kingdom in increasingly dramatic terms. He then must have appeared a greater and greater threat. If language such as "messiah" and even "Davidic ruler" were also heard, the urgency to take action must have increased.

At the same time, interest in Jesus among the crowds would have grown. He most likely became something of a celebrity. Mark may have touched on the actual situation when he reports that "they wanted to arrest him, but they feared the crowd" (12:12; see Mt 21:46; Lk 20:19). It is thus reasonable to conclude that the leadership began to plan how to destroy Jesus: "The chief priests and the scribes were looking for a way to arrest Jesus by stealth and kill him" (Mk 14:1; Mt 26:3–4; Lk 22:2). John, probably more accurately, has the plot hatched earlier in that Holy Week (11:50–53). There seems no reason to doubt that at the core of the growing opposition we have "history remembered."

The four gospels are in agreement: "Then Judas Iscariot, who was one of the twelve, went to the chief priests in order to betray him to them" (Mk 14:10; Mt 26:14–16; Lk 22:3–6; Jn 13:2). John offers the explanation for the betrayal: "He was a thief; he kept the common purse and used to steal what was put into it" (12:6). Whatever the motivation, it is highly unlikely that the evangelists or earlier Christians would have created the embarrassing report that Jesus was betrayed by one of his own followers. Speaking of other scripture scholars, Brown affirms that "relatively few would deny that Judas betrayed Jesus."[9]

It is understandable that the gospel traditions accord Jesus full knowledge of what is to happen. Even Mark, who stresses Jesus' humanity by showing his limitations, has the following: "Then [Jesus] began to teach them that the Son of Man must undergo great suffering, and be rejected by the elders, the chief priests, and the scribes, and be killed, and after three days rise again" (8:31). Without according Jesus such detailed knowledge, we still could credit him with some awareness of his impending fate. He could hardly have been ignorant of the power of his enemies, especially in Jerusalem. Could Jesus have been unaware that persistence in challenging the authorities would have the direst consequences? Was he, like those overwhelmingly committed to a cause, unwilling or unable to desist whatever the threat? We have seen such individuals throughout human history. Some are called fanatics, others saints.

V. THE LAST SUPPER

A. A Final Meal

With the exception of the nativity and the crucifixion no scene is more enshrined in the Christian memory than that of the Last Supper. Moreover, the core religious ritual of most Christian groups is built around the memory of Jesus' final meal with his apostles. Everything indicates that this liturgical tradition reaches back to a very early stage of Christianity's history. Joachim Jeremias says the tradition "belongs therefore to *the first decade after the death of Jesus,*"[10] and that *"at the beginning there stands not liturgy but historical account."*[11] Meier agrees, saying, "The historicity of a final farewell meal held by Jesus with his disciples is generally accepted by scholars across the spectrum."[12]

B. A Passover Meal?

1. CONFLICTING ACCOUNTS

It is one thing to affirm that the Jesus of history joined with some of his followers for a meal that proved to be his last; it is another to determine what happened at that meal. Here we confront a most difficult challenge in interpreting the gospel record. Mark, followed by Matthew and Luke, is quite clear: "On the first day of Unleavened Bread, when the Passover lamb is sacrificed, his disciples said to him, 'Where do you want us to go and make the preparations for you to eat the Passover?'" (14:12; Mt 26:17; Lk 22:7–9). It follows, then, that Jesus would have been subsequently tried and executed on the day of Passover.

To the contrary, we are told in the gospel of John that when the Jewish leaders brought Jesus before Pilate "it was early in the morning [Friday]. They themselves did not enter the headquarters, so as to avoid ritual defilement and to be able to eat the Passover" (18:28). This is reiterated later when the gospel dates the execution of Jesus: "Now it was the day of Preparation for the Passover" (19:14). In the Johannine chronology the meal on the previous evening could not have been the traditional celebration of Passover.

2. SUPPORT FOR THE SYNOPTIC CHRONOLOGY

Scholars have labored mightily to reconcile these two conflicting versions, but to no avail. "None of these attempts at harmonization therefore is convincing....The question remains an open one: Was the Last Supper of Jesus a passover meal or not?"[13] Nevertheless, Jeremias holds that there is evidence supporting the synoptic chronology. He cites verses in the Marcan account supporting the contention that the final meal Jesus shared with his followers was a Passover celebration. The following is a summary of Jeremias's view.[14]

Jesus and his companions customarily left the city each evening for nearby Bethany (Mk 11:11–12; 14:3). On Thursday evening they did not. An explanation would be that the Passover meal was traditionally celebrated within the confines of Jerusalem. As it was also the tradition to remain in the city for the night of Passover, we may have the reason the group went to Gethsemane rather than returning to Bethany.[15]

All the accounts agree that the final meal was eaten at night.[16] This was contrary to the normal practice of the period, which was to eat the day's final meal in the afternoon. By tradition, however, the Passover meal was eaten at night (Ex 12:8).

We also have agreement among the sources that Jesus and his companions *reclined* at table.[17] Indeed, the scene in John only makes sense if Peter and the disciple "whom Jesus loved" were reclining on either side of Jesus (13:23–25). It is an odd detail for such unanimity. Yet there was the custom that during the Passover meal the Jews reclined rather than sat at table as a symbol of their freedom from slavery, a Passover theme.

Abstracting for the moment from the eucharistic elements in the Last Supper, three items also indicate something special about the meal itself. The synoptics agree that Jesus broke and distributed some bread during the supper. It was the usual custom to do this at the *beginning* of the meal by way of a blessing. In the Passover celebration it was done *during* the supper as part of the ritual. In addition, wine was shared among the participants. For Jesus' contemporaries wine was not a part of ordinary meals. At Passover, in contrast, four cups of wine were shared. Finally, the meal concluded with a hymn, again, not part of an ordinary meal but characteristic of the Passover ritual.[18]

Jeremias closes his discussion of the chronology conflict with: "Of absolutely decisive significance is one last observation."[19] It is that Jesus announced his impending passion by *"speaking words of interpretation over the bread and the wine."*[20] This is crucial because *"interpretation of the special elements of the meal is a fixed part of the passover ritual."*[21] An ordinary meal would not have provided such a framework for what was a central part of the synoptic tradition.

> So when the Synoptic gospels nevertheless describe the Last Supper as a passover meal and do not allow it to be lost in the tradition, the reason is obviously that the recollection of the fact was too firmly established to be removed by the influence of ritual practice. We have here, then, "survival of an historical reminiscence."[22]

As we see, Jeremias regards elements of the Last Supper as "history remembered."

How do we explain, then, the contrary Johannine chronology? There is an early tradition—and a popular one—that compared Jesus to the Paschal lamb.[23] According to Jeremias: "It was quite possibly the popularity and vividness of this comparison which affect the recollection of the events of the Passion and caused them to be antedated by twenty-four hours"[24] in some early traditions. Also, the growing alienation between Christians and Jews as the first century ended might have suppressed the memory of Jesus celebrating Passover. That alienation is particularly influential in the gospel of John.

C. The Eucharistic Words

In accepting Jeremias's conclusion we have Jesus and his companions sharing the Passover's ritual meal. The meal is celebratory: the food is ample, and the wine flows freely. The time-honored epic of Israel's freedom from slavery is retold as the meal progresses. We cannot accurately re-create the ritual as it was at the time of Jesus. With what evidence we have, Jeremias outlines that ritual as follows:

A. Preliminary Course:

Words of dedication...spoken by the paterfamilias over the first cup (the *kiddush* cup).

Preliminary dish, consisting...of green herbs, bitter herbs and a sauce made of fruit purée.

The meal proper (see C) is served but not eaten; the second cup is mixed [wine was usually mixed with water before drinking] and put in place but not yet drunk.

B. Passover Liturgy:

Passover *haggadah*[25] by the paterfamilias (in Aramaic).

First part of the passover *hallel* (in Hebrew).[26]

Drinking of the second cup (*haggadah* cup).

C. The Main Meal:

Grace spoken by the paterfamilias over the unleavened bread.

Meal, consisting of passover lamb, unleavened bread, bitter herbs (Exodus 12:8), with fruit purée.

Grace *(birkat hammason)* over the third cup (cup of blessing).

D. Conclusion:

Second part of the passover *hallel* (in Hebrew).

Praise over the fourth cup (*hallel* cup).[27]

The tradition is that Jesus, at certain moments in the celebration, introduced additional comments into the ceremony. Luke's account may be the closest to the original sequence:

[Jesus] said to them, "I have eagerly desired to eat this Passover with you before I suffer; for I tell you, I will not eat it until it is fulfilled in the kingdom of God." Then he took a cup, and after giving thanks he said, "Take this and divide it among yourselves; for I tell you that from now on I will not drink of the fruit of the vine until the kingdom of God comes." Then he took a loaf of bread, and when he had given thanks, he broke it and gave it to them, saying, "This is my body, which is given for you. Do this in remembrance of me." And he did the same with the cup after supper, saying, "This cup that is poured out for you is the new covenant in my blood." (22:15–20)[28]

Viewing these additions Jeremias observes: "But above all we shall see that *Jesus' avowal of abstinence, the words of interpretation and the command to repetition first become fully understandable when they are set within the context of the passover ritual.*"[29] Jesus, increasingly aware that his ministry was to come to a calamitous end, sought to prepare his followers by these variations in that ritual.

D. Avowal of Abstinence

It would certainly have startled Jesus' companions when, at the beginning of the meal, he proclaimed: "I have eagerly desired to eat this Passover with you before I suffer, for I tell you, I will not eat it until it is fulfilled in the kingdom of God" (Lk 22:15–16). Then raising the *kiddush* cup (see above), he continues: "Take this and divide it among yourselves; for I tell you that from now on I will not drink of the fruit of the vine until the kingdom of God comes" (22:17–18). As Jeremias concludes, "At the Last Supper therefore Jesus neither ate of the passover lamb nor drank of the wine; probably he fasted completely."[30]

We have already noted Jesus' conviction that the coming of God's kingdom was imminent. What Jeremias is basically saying here is: "The next meal of Jesus with his disciples will be the Messianic meal on a transformed earth."[31] There is evidence that his disciples got the message. Apparently some of the earliest Christian communities reflected Jesus' action by themselves fasting on the night of the Jewish Passover.[32]

E. The Words of Interpretation

1. THE WORDS

During the Passover *haggadah* the special elements of the meal are interpreted in the light of the Exodus events. It is a custom, still part of the Jewish Seder, that the youngest one at table asks the traditional questions. Then, at the beginning of the meal proper, the paterfamilias, Jesus in this case, "took a loaf of bread, and when he had given thanks, he broke it and gave it to them, saying, 'This is my body, which is given for you.'" The blessing, giving thanks, was most likely: "Praised be thou, O Lord, our God, King of the world, who causes bread to come forth from the earth."[33]

The Passover meal now followed. There is a persistent memory that Jesus' betrayer, Judas Iscariot, was present at the meal but left before it ended.[34] It might be that Judas, fully understanding the import of what Jesus was saying, decided to profit from what he now saw as a hopeless situation.

The Passover meal itself concluded with the sharing in the "cup of blessing" *(birkat hammason)* and a blessing by the paterfamilias. Then, as Luke tells us: "And he did the same with the cup after supper, saying, 'This cup that is poured out for you is the new covenant in my blood'" (22:20). The concluding parts of the ritual follow. Mark (14:26) followed by Matthew (26:30) preserve the memory of the "second part of the passover *hallel*" in reporting: "When they had sung the hymn, they went out to the Mount of Olives."

2. THE INTERPRETATION

In Paul's first letter to the Corinthians we have the earliest version of Jesus' words of interpretation: "This is my body that is for you....This cup is the new covenant in my blood" (11:24–25). If we grant that the Jesus of history did pronounce these words or similar ones, what might he have meant to convey to his hearers? Jeremias reminds us:

> But it is of the greatest importance to remember that Jesus' words of interpretation were not for his disciples, as they are for us, something isolated, but that they were prepared for by the interpretations which Jesus, following the normal custom, had given to the special elements of the meal during the mediation.[35]

The focus then was on the bread that was broken and the wine that was poured.

> It was not the action of breaking the bread or of pouring out the wine that Jesus interpreted but rather *the bread and the wine itself.*...Its meaning is quite simple. Each one of the disciples could understand it. Jesus made the broken bread a simile of the fate of his body, the blood of the grapes a simile of his outpoured blood. "I go to death as the true passover sacrifice."[36]

Convinced that his fate was sealed Jesus prepared his followers for what was to come. Jeremias concludes:

> Only the fact of his vicarious death is announced by Jesus in the simile, not the details of its manner. Nonetheless we can see from the simile...that Jesus did expect a violent death....Jesus was certain that God would vindicate his death by his resurrection and the establishment of the kingdom.[37]

F. Repetition Is Commanded

Writing to the Christian community in Corinth, Paul reminds them: "The cup of blessing that we bless, is it not a sharing in the blood of Christ? The bread that we break, is it not a sharing in the body of Christ?" (2 Cor 10:16). He also, as we saw above, records the earliest version of the eucharistic liturgy. The Book of Acts indicates that in the earliest times Christians, while still observing the Jewish rituals, gathered for their own celebrations: "They devoted themselves to the apostles' teaching and fellowship, to the breaking of bread and the prayers" (2:42). In doing so, it is possible that they were carrying out a directive given by Jesus to his follower at their final meal.

In Paul's recounting of the Last Supper, after each of the words of interpretation, Jesus directs his disciples to repeat the ritual, saying, "Do this in remembrance of me" (1 Cor 11:24–25). Though Jesus and the earliest Christians may have thought the time remaining before the Apocalypse was short, the remembrance could still have been something Jesus mandated.

G. Conclusion

Mark, followed by Matthew, has the scene of Last Supper end with the singing of a hymn, possibly the "second part of the passover *hallel,*" as mentioned above (Mk 14:26; Mt 26:30). With that, Jesus and his party leave the city for the Mount of Olives. Luke agrees on the destination (22:39).[38] It is the place from which Jesus began his entry into the city four days earlier (Mk 11:1; Mt 21:1; Lk 19:29). Here we may have "prophecy historicized" rather than "history remembered."

There are a number of references to the locale in the Hebrew Bible. Perhaps the one that influences the evangelists most is King David's leaving of the city upon his betrayal by his son Absalom (2 Sm 15:30ff.). It is not coincidental that, at this point, Jesus predicts his abandonment by his followers, included Peter (Mk 14:27–31; Mt 26:31–35). The contrast between Jesus entering the city as a triumphant Davidic monarch and now seen as the betrayed regal figure was not lost on the evangelists.

Chapter Ten

ARREST AND INTERROGATION

I. PASSION NARRATIVE

In his 1994 work *The Death of the Messiah: From Gethsemane to the Grave,* Raymond Brown begins his treatment of the passion narrative *after* the final supper Jesus had with his disciples. Many scholars would include the Last Supper as part of that narrative. Brown justifies his delineation as dictated not "by scholarly consensus but by practicality."[1] Considering that *The Death of the Messiah* comprises two volumes we can see his point.

The synoptic chronology, following Mark, has Jesus go from the Mount of Olives to a nearby olive grove called Gethsemane. He and his companions were to spend the night. Sometime later, possibly after midnight, Jesus was arrested and taken to the residence of the high priest, presumably in Jerusalem (14:43, 53). After being interrogated and condemned, Jesus was turned over to the Roman procurator, Pontius Pilate (15:1).[2]

Pilate sentenced Jesus to death by crucifixion (15:15). Jesus was then taken under guard to a site identified as Golgotha (15:22), most certainly located outside the city. There the sentence was carried out at "nine o'clock in the morning" (15:25). At noon, there was an astronomical phenomenon, described as "darkness" coming over the whole land (15:33). At three o'clock Jesus died (15:34, 37), and sometime prior to sunset and the beginning of the sabbath, he was buried in a nearby tomb (15:42, 46). No activities are reported for the following day. Then, on the first day of the week, the tomb was found to be empty (16:1–8).

John is in substantial agreement with the synoptic chronology, save for placing Jesus' execution on the day before Passover.

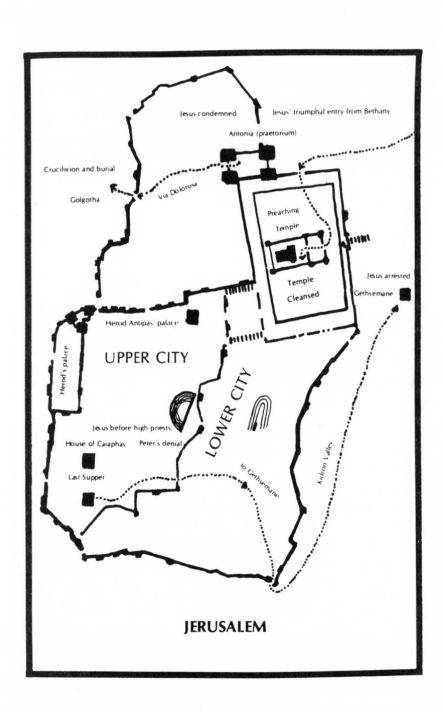

Jesus condemned

Jesus' triumphal entry from Bethany

Antonia (praetorium)

Crucifixion and burial

Golgotha

Via Dolorosa

Preaching

Temple

Temple
Cleansed

Jesus arrested

Gethsemane

Herod Antipas' palace

Herod's palace

UPPER CITY

LOWER CITY

Jesus before high priests:

House of Caiaphas

Peter's denial

to Gethsemane

Kidron Valley

Last Supper

JERUSALEM

II. THE GARDEN EPISODE

A. *Jesus' Prayer*

In an article in the *Biblical Archaeology Review* (July/August 1995) Joan E. Taylor proposes that Gethsemane (the word is probably related to the Aramaic for "oil press") was not a garden, as it is usually described, but rather a nearby cave in which there was an actual olive press. Brown notes that since the place "has no known theological import, there is good reason to regard 'Gethsemane' as coming from early tradition and, indeed, as a historical reminiscence."[3] John's gospel adds a crucial note: "Now Judas, who betrayed him, also knew the place, because Jesus often met there with his disciples" (18:2).

We discussed earlier the prayer of Jesus in Gethsemane as giving us some knowledge of his characteristic manner of praying. We can, however, come to no conclusion as to the historicity of the scene itself.

> I posit that early Christians had a tradition that before he died Jesus struggled in prayer about his fate....They fleshed out the prayer tradition in the light of the psalms and of their own prayers, both of which they associated with Jesus' way of praying.[4]

The struggle, as pictured in the synoptics,[5] is not flattering to Jesus and thus not likely to have been created by the early Christian tradition. Rather, it would seem, his reported anguish was "history remembered."

B. *The Arrest*

As noted earlier, Jesus was betrayed by a follower, Judas Iscariot. The gospels all agree that Judas led the arresting party to Gethsemane.[6] The makeup of the party is not so clear. The synoptics speak of an armed "crowd"; John seems to have in mind a more organized unit; "a detachment of soldiers together with police." They are acting under the authority of the "chief priests," "elders," "scribes," "captains of the temple" and "Pharisees." In the synoptics, apparently to prevent a case of mistaken identity, Judas singles out Jesus with a kiss (Mk 14:44–45; Mt 26:48–49; Lk 22:48). John omits this touch; he has Jesus identify himself (18:5).

When Jesus is seized by the arresting party the synoptics report that one among Jesus' followers struck "the slave of the high priest and cut off his ear" (Mk 14:47; Mt 26:51; Lk 22:50). John identifies the attacker as Simon Peter and the slave as a Malchus (18:10), making it, in Brown's words, "the best attested single section of the whole Mount of Olives sequence!"[7] The gesture is futile, and Jesus is led off. Mark records the stark fact that Jesus' followers deserted him at this point (14:50).[8] "Most critics see no reason to doubt that this belonged to the earliest tradition of the [passion narrative], and indeed there is little reason for doubting factuality."[9]

The Jesus of history—agonizing in the face of what he suspects is coming, betrayed by a friend, seized by an armed party sent by his enemies and abandoned by his companions—is led off captive in the dead of night; all this is undoubtedly "history remembered."

III. THE JEWISH INTERROGATION OF JESUS

A. The Sanhedrin

It is customary to speak of the appearance of Jesus before the Jerusalem leadership and his subsequent appearance before Pilate as *trials*. However, just how formal either of these proceedings was is an open question. *Interrogation* is a more general and thus better term.

The synoptics follow Mark: "They took Jesus to the high priest; and all the chief priests, the elders, and the scribes were assembled" (14:53). The assembly appears to have been the Sanhedrin.[10] As we read in Brown:

> Thus most scholars have little difficulty in positing that during the Roman prefecture in Judea a Sanhedrin...of priests, elders and scribes, led by the chief priests, played a major administrative and judicial role in Jewish self-governance in Judea.[11]

Matthew supplies the additional note that the high priest was Caiaphas, whom we know served in that post from 18 to 36 C.E.[12]

As noted, the Temple leadership had determined to deal with Jesus and authorized his arrest (Mk 14:1; Mt 26:3–4; Lk 22:2). John places this meeting several weeks prior to Jesus' final visit to Jerusalem. "Historically, having a Sanhedrin session weeks before Passover would be more plausible than one gathered hastily in the middle of the night."[13]

Moreover, we know little of this body's rules of conduct. Brown notes: "In the literature written before A.D. 100, when the Sanhedrin does sentence to death, there is little evidence of courtlike procedures to protect the defendant....Perhaps all that can be said is that the trial of Jesus recounted in the gospels would not clearly violate the written Law in most of its details."[14] It is obvious that whatever took place on that fateful night, the result was a foregone conclusion.

B. The Charge

The crucial question is asked by the high priest: "Are you the Messiah, the Son of the Blessed One?"[15] When Jesus replies affirmatively, the reaction is immediate: "Then the high priest tore his clothes and said, 'Why do we still need witnesses? You have heard his blasphemy! What is your decision? All of them condemned him as deserving death."[16] Do we have any reason to believe that Jesus was condemned in such a manner? The plausibility of such an occurrence rests on whether or not we can find something in Jesus' life that would merit the charge.

C. The Messiah

When the title Messiah was discussed above, it was judged unlikely that "publicly or privately Jesus clearly claimed to be the Messiah." On the other hand, "it [is] plausible that during Jesus' lifetime some of his followers thought him to be the Messiah." Further, it is "very likely" that "Jesus' opponents (Roman or Jewish) interpreted (honestly or dishonestly) him or his followers as making the claim that he was the Messiah."[17] Here we may well find the basis for the ultimate charge against Jesus that he was a royal claimant. But would being a messianic claimant serve as grounds for the charge of blasphemy? Brown does not think it likely.[18]

D. Son of God or Son of Man?

What of the title "son of God"? Could it be the basis of the accusation? Again, Brown believes such an assumption can be ruled out: "It is unlikely that title was used of Jesus during his lifetime either by himself or by his followers."[19] If, as Vermes holds, the title was in fact used, it was only used in the sense of Jesus being admired as a just and saintly man.

In Mark, it is Jesus' self-identification as the son of man that appears to trigger the charge of blasphemy:

"You will see the Son of Man
seated at the right hand of the Power,
and coming with the clouds of heaven" (14:62; Mt 26:64).

Moreover, as we saw earlier, the title son of man is one Jesus did use in his lifetime.[20] Could that title serve as a basis for the accusation of blasphemy? It is Brown's conclusion that "one would be imprudent to base the historicity of the Jewish charge of blasphemy on that alone."[21]

E. Threat to the Temple

Why the lethal hostility toward Jesus on the part of Judea's officialdom? We have already pointed out how a rural Hasid challenging the legalistic approach to observance of the Law engendered the opposition of the Pharisees, a group not without influence in the capital city. Was there something else that would have been more specifically threatening to the chief priests and their supporters? A clue may lie in the remark false accusers attribute to Jesus: "We heard him say, 'I will destroy this temple that is made with hands, and in three days I will build another, not made with hands'" (Mk 14:58).[22]

We have already spoken of Jesus' cleansing of the Temple, a dramatic gesture highlighting perceived abuses of that greatest of all religious centers. Looking forward, as he was, to the immanent coming of God's kingdom, Jesus, when speaking of the Temple, might well have said: "Do you see these great buildings? Not one stone will be left here upon another; all will be thrown down" (Mk 13:2). Moreover, Jesus' general attitude of distrust toward wealth and his stress of a total dependence of God could have resulted in his appearing to threaten to the status quo. Brown says, "I would join those scholars, then, who give a very high probability to Jesus having spoken about the forth coming destruction and rebuilding of the sanctuary."[23] Though it was the source of Jewish officialdom's opposition to Jesus, a threat to the Temple is not the charge actually leveled against Jesus; he was accused of blasphemy.

F. Jesus' Ministry

In the end it may not be possible to determine the grounds for the blasphemy charge on the record we have of the Sanhedrin interrogation. Perhaps a broader canvas is needed. We have already seen that Jesus' ministry had engendered opposition from almost the beginning. He is said to have spoken "with authority," but without the usual credentials. He claimed the power to forgive sin, which some of his hearers believed was something only God could do. He backed his claims by "deeds of power," which some regarded as demonic. "Jesus took a stance on the Law, especially concerning the Sabbath, that would have seemed highly disputable to the Sadducees, Pharisee, or Essenes."[24] We have already noted his criticism of the Temple and the possibility of his public demonstration within the sacred precincts. Summing up, Brown notes, "I see little reason to doubt that his opponents would have considered him blasphemous."[25] Thus, they would have had religious grounds for condemnation.

IV. INTERIM

The synoptic gospels agree with Mark's report of Jesus being abused and mocked by some of those present at the interrogation (Mk 14:65; Mt 26:67–68; Lk 22:63–65). John reports only abuse, however (18:22). Brown comments, "Such abuse is not at all implausible historically."[26] We can say the same of Peter's denial of being associated with or even knowing Jesus of Nazareth.[27] Brown affirms that the incident "was irradically established as tradition."[28] Thus the reported abuse can be reckoned as "history remembered."[29]

V. JESUS TRANSFERRED TO PILATE

The transfer of Jesus from the jurisdiction of the Sanhedrin to that of the Roman procurator is attested to by all four gospels.[30] Such a transfer bears out the testimony of Josephus and Tacitus that Jesus was executed at the orders of Pilate. As chance has it, there is a historical record of such an action by the Judean leadership.

In the early 60s C.E., at a celebration of Tabernacles, "one Jeshua, son of Ananias, a very ordinary yokel,...stood in the Temple and began to shout '...a voice against Jerusalem and the Sanctuary....'"[31] We are told that the Jewish authorities, upset by these rantings, took the man before the Roman procurator. The latter, believing the man to be insane, had him flogged and then released. It is quite possible that some thirty years earlier a like transfer took place under similar circumstances.

The question remains: Having condemned Jesus to death, why did the Sanhedrin not carry out the sentence? Only John's gospel offers an explanation: "Pilate said to them, 'Take him yourselves and judge him according to your law.' The Jews replied, 'We are not permitted to put anyone to death'" (18:31). Was there in fact such a limitation on the power of the Judean authorities?

We can see in the example just cited the possibility that the Jewish authorities wanted to execute "Jeshua" but did not do so. Brown concludes:

> The Romans permitted the Jews to execute for certain clear religious offenses....Beyond this specified religious sphere the Jewish authorities were supposed to hand over cases to the Romans, who would decide whether or not to pass and execute a death sentence.[32]

The Jesus of history now stood before an imperial tribunal.

VI. THE ROMAN INTERROGATION

A. Pontius Pilate

At the point in time when the gospels took their final form, 70 to 90 C.E., Christians were largely Gentiles living in the cities of the Roman Empire. They had experienced the hostility of the Jewish communities, which, no doubt, influenced how they recalled Jesus' treatment by the Jewish leadership. These Christians were also confronted with the inescapable knowledge that Christianity's founder was executed by order of a Roman official. There were Christians who stood accused before similar civil officials. In the light of these circumstances the gospels' portrayal of the encounter between Jesus and Pilate will touch on extremely sensitive matters.

In many ways the key to picturing the Jesus of history at this crucial juncture is the character of the man he stands before. The Roman procurator, Pontius Pilate, was himself a figure of conflicting depictions, as the references in Josephus, Tacitus and Philo[33] reveal. How does the gospel presentation fit into these other views of the procurator? Brown holds that the New Testament "descriptions are not patently implausible....The theory that the Gospels exculpate the Romans by creating a fictional, sympathetic Pilate has been overdone."[34] The gospel record may well tone down some aspects of the procurator, yet without departing too far from his actual treatment of Jesus.[35]

B. The Interrogation

Normally, the governor or procurator of Judea administered the province from his headquarters in Caesarea Maritima on the coast of the Mediterranean. However, on such occasions as Passover, he and his entourage moved up to Jerusalem. There are two places where he would have been headquartered: the Fortress Antonia, attached to the Temple area, or the Herodian Palace. The latter is the more likely.

All the gospels agree on the crucial question Pilate put to Jesus: "Are you the King of the Jews?" Jesus' answer is ambiguous: "You say so."[36] In each of the gospels the Greek for these passages is identical, clear evidence of the antiquity of the tradition. If the question reflects "history remembered," what might have led Pilate to ask it?

We have already noted that the kingdom of God was a central theme in Jesus' message, perhaps becoming more so as his ministry ended. The Roman authorities could have understood that language to refer to the reestablishment of an independent rule over Judea and Jerusalem. The "nail in the coffin," as it were, could have been the title of Messiah, which we saw earlier was possibly stressed by Jesus' enemies.

The suspicion that Jesus was claiming to be a "new David" would have aroused the concern of any Roman procurator. As Brown puts it:

> Thus in first-century Palestine the charge that Jesus was claiming the title might well be understood by the Romans as an attempt to reestablish the kingship over Judea and Jerusalem exercised by the Hasmonaeans (like Alexander Jannaeus) and Herod the Great.[37]

Around this kernel of history each evangelist has woven an account of Jesus' interrogation by Pilate. Mark's is the simplest; Matthew's and

Luke's add further details; John gives us the most elaborate.[38] These accounts are largely in agreement. In each gospel Pilate is shown to be skeptical of the charge and seeks to free Jesus—and in each yields to the outcry of a crowd.[39]

We know from Josephus that Pilate on a number of occasions bowed to the wishes of a crowd of Jews who were demonstrating. Brown notes that "the bullying of Pilate by his Jewish adversaries in the incident of the shields resembles strongly the bullying of Pilate in John's account of the passion, including the threat of appeal to the emperor."[40] Again we have strong evidence of "history remembered."

C. Barabbas

A striking feature of the trial of Jesus before Pilate is the role of a man named Barabbas. Mark has the basic account: "Now at the festival [Pilate] used to release a prisoner for them, anyone for whom they asked. Now a man called Barabbas was in prison with the rebels who had committed murder during the insurrection" (15:6–7). Pilate offers to release Jesus on the occasion. "For he realized that it was out of jealousy that the chief priests had handed him over. But the chief priests stirred up the crowd to have him release Barabbas for them instead" (15:10–11).

Matthew speaks of "a notorious prisoner, called Jesus Barabbas" (27:16). Luke, speaking of Barabbas, says, "This was a man who had been put in prison for an insurrection that had taken place in the city, and for murder" (23:19). John writes simply, "Now Barabbas was a bandit" (18:40). The agreement among the gospels strongly indicates "history remembered," especially in the case of Mark and John. The nature of that history is sharply debated. Brown concludes: "It is far less demanding on the imagination to posit that historically a real man with a patronymic 'son of Abba' and a personal name Jesus was arrested during a riot in Jerusalem but spared by Pilate."[41]

We are left, however, the question of the historicity of the custom of releasing a prisoner at Passover. Roman officials, such as Pilate, could certainly grant pardons if they wished to do so. Yet it is doubtful that it would have been done as a matter of custom, say on the occasion of a religious celebration. Perhaps the best solution is that there was a Jesus Barabbas pardoned by Pilate but not in connection with the trial of

Jesus. Later, the contrast between someone guilty being spared and an innocent condemned struck early followers of Jesus of Nazareth who knew of both events. The tradition later wove the two events together. The fact that both men had the same personal name may well have facilitated the process.

D. *Jesus Is Condemned to Death*

Finally, as each of the gospels records, Pilate yielded to the crowd's demands and ordered Jesus to be crucified. There is no question that the procurator had the power to give such an order, and he, in the case of non-Roman citizens, was not necessarily limited to the legal niceties. In 41 C.E., when Herod Agrippa took over from Pilate, who had been recalled to Rome, he accused his predecessor of "constantly repeated executions without trial."[42] One such execution could have been that of Jesus, the Nazorean.

Traumatic as the decision of Pilate may have been to Jesus' followers at the time, and as history-shaking turned out to be, it was in the procurator's career a matter of little note. A Jew is brought before him by the Judean leadership. They accuse him of royal aspirations. Pilate may have suspected there were other reasons, but whatever were his hesitations, an outcry from a "crowd" dispelled them and he rendered a condemnation, probably without further thought.

The experiences of the early Christians with both the Jews and with Roman officialdom certainly colored the gospel accounts. Yet it should be noted that the depictions of Jesus' interrogations reflect the words of Josephus we quoted earlier: "Pilate, because of an accusation made by leading men among us, condemned him to the cross." Whatever the actual course of events, the Jesus of history faced the cruelest and most degrading of punishments inflicted by the empire on its enemies.

Chapter Eleven

THE DEATH OF JESUS

I. INTRODUCTION

A. *The Fact of the Crucifixion*

We come now to the scene most vividly fixed in the Christian imagination, the crucifixion of Jesus. Yet it was not until centuries after the actual event that the cross became a Christian symbol, and it was even later that the *corpus* was shown upon that cross. The reason is not difficult to discern. Until the fourth century C.E. crucifixion was the usual form of punishment the empire imposed on slaves and others. However, it was regarded as so degrading that it could not be imposed on Roman citizens. Few of the early Christians would have been spared the sight of an unfortunate gasping away his life in such an horrific manner. They hardly wanted reminders that Jesus died in that way.

Yet it was a fact that could hardly have been disputed. The event is reported by prestigious historians of the period. Josephus writes: "Pilate, because of an accusation made by leading men among us, condemned him [Jesus] to the cross."[1] Tacitus speaks of a "Christ, who, during the reign of Tiberias, had been executed by the procurator Pontius Pilate."[2] No doubt Jesus' crucifixion was a matter of acute embarrassment to his earliest followers.

Nor did their adversaries, Jew and Gentile alike, let them forget it. A crude drawing, dating from as late as the third century C.E., has been found in Rome. It shows a crucified figure with a donkey's head and is entitled "Alexamenos worships his god." In face of such mockery the evangelists confronted the formidable task of making the way in which Jesus died understandable to their readers.

B. Limits to Our Knowledge

Can history tell us any more than that Jesus was crucified? At one extreme is John Dominic Crossan: "In conclusion, I cannot find any detailed historical information about the crucifixion of Jesus." Not one to spare the reader Crossan concludes:

> What is the historicity of the burial? From Roman expectations, the body of Jesus and of any others crucified with him would have been left on the cross as carrion for the crows and the dogs.[3]

Details beyond the fact of Jesus' crucifixion Crossan regards as items added to explain that death, usually as "prophecy historicized." Again, while not vouching for the historicity of every aspect of the gospels' accounts, less radical authors, such as Raymond Brown and John P. Meier, give a greater role to "history remembered."

True, the evangelists themselves did not witness the death of Jesus. "Yet as we move back from the gospel narratives to Jesus himself, ultimately there were eyewitnesses and earwitnesses who were in position to know the broad lines of Jesus' passion."[4] Speaking of those who were followers of Jesus during his public life, Brown states:

> It is inconceivable that they showed no concern about what happened to Jesus after his death....It is absurd to think that some information was not available to them about why Jesus was hanged on the cross....There was no massive Christian indifference as to what actually happened at the end of Jesus life.[5]

Recovering that historical substrate in our search for the details of Jesus' death will not be easy. We will have to recognize with Brown "the likely existence of history and tradition behind the heavily scripturally reflective, kerygmatically oriented, and theologically organized [passion narrative] of the Gospels."[6] As Brown points out: "An essential step, then, in appreciating the import of Mark's [passion narrative] is to recognize the effects of selection, compression, simplification, sharpening, and dramatization."[7] We see the same process at work in Matthew and Luke, each making use of Mark and his individual tradition in the same manner.[8]

II. CARRYING THE CROSS

Mark records that Jesus was flogged after his condemnation (15:15–20) and then mocked by the soldiers who were to carry out the sentence, as does Matthew (27:26–31). John mentions these events as occurring earlier (19:1–3). This scourging and mockery and abuse may have been the memory of what was the common fate of such unfortunates. As Brown observes, "The content of what is described in the Gospels about the Roman mockery is not implausible."[9]

It was apparently the custom for the condemned man to carry his cross. This did not mean the entire cruciform object as usually depicted, but only the horizontal crossbeam. The upright section was already in place at the site of the execution. Jesus, however, may not have carried his means of execution unassisted. The synoptic gospels are clear that Jesus was aided by one Simon of Cyrene, albeit unwillingly.[10] Mark tells us that Simon was the father of Alexander and Rufus, a duo who must have been known to his community (15:21). The motivation for enlisting Simon was not likely to have been kindness but rather the fear that Jesus might not survive to be executed. Brown finds nothing implausible about this memory of Simon.[11]

III. THE CRUCIFIXION

A. The Tradition

The basic details are found in Mark:

> Then they brought Jesus to the place called Golgotha (which means the place of a skull). And they offered him wine mixed with myrrh; but he did not take it. And they crucified him, and divided his clothes among them, casting lots to decide what each should take.
>   It was nine o'clock in the morning when they crucified him. The inscription of the charge against him read, "The King of the Jews." And with him they crucified two bandits, one on his right and one on his left. (15:22–27)

The synoptic gospels are in general agreement with the details cited in Mark (Mt 27:33–38; Lk 23:33–34, 38). John's gospel agrees with Mark on a number of points: the site of the execution was "Golgotha";

Jesus was crucified with two others; the charge was "King of the Jews"; Jesus was offered something to drink; his clothes were divided among his executioners (19:17–23). Also, the synoptics, following Mark (15:40–41), and John (19:25) indicate that there were women present at the execution. We have here further indication that the two evangelists may have shared an earlier tradition.

B. The Place

Historical records and archeological findings indicate that an abandoned quarry was located outside a gate in the city walls as they existed in the first century C.E.[12] A skull-like mound of unquarried stone within the quarry may well have given the place its name. It is also possible that tombs had been cut into the sides of the quarry. If the area was used regularly by the authorities for executions, upright stakes would have been permanently in place, possible on top of the mound itself.

C. The Offering of Wine

All the gospels agree that at some point Jesus was offered wine to drink. Mark (15:23) and Matthew (27:34) place the gesture at the beginning of the scene; Luke (23:36) and John (15:29–30) have it occurring later on. It also should be noted that Mark (15:36) and Matthew (27:48) have as second offering of wine that appears to correspond with that of Luke and John. The gospels seem to agree that Jesus was offered a drink of *oxos,* a vinegarized wine, the common beverage of the less affluent. It might have been offered to Jesus as an act of kindness. Mark speaks of "wine mixed with myrrh," which could have been held out to Jesus in an effort to ease his pain. Some such incident would be "history remembered."

However, "prophecy historicized" cannot be ruled out. We have the passage from Psalm 69:

> They gave me poison for food,
> and for my thirst they gave me vinegar to drink. (v. 21)

The psalm is credited to King David and depicts the monarch in great distress, being persecuted by his enemies. In specifying "sour wine," each of the gospels could be reflecting an early Christian use of the psalm to make the sufferings of Jesus, seen as a Davidic figure, more understandable.

D. The Crucifixion

The crucifixion of Jesus is probably the most familiar scene in all of history. Yet, the gospels simply state, with little detail, that it happened.[13] One likely reason for the brevity is that early followers of Jesus were all too familiar with the empire's most used form of public execution. Second, as already noted, the manner of Jesus' death was of considerable embarrassment to the early Christians. Thus, Jesus' mode of execution, evaluated by Josephus as "the most pitiable of deaths,"[14] was recounted with as little explicit description as possible.

Brown believes it to be "historically plausible" that Jesus was attached to the crossbeam by nails driven through his wrists.[15] Then the beam itself was placed on the upright, and his feet were attached to the upright. A recent discovery in Palestine reveals that the feet of a crucified victim were drawn up under him and his heels nailed to the upright. Such a procedure would have given the unfortunate the support that would prolong his life. The manner in which Jesus was fastened to the cross must have resulted in an agony that almost exceeds imagination.

E. The Division of His Clothes

Each of the gospels reports the division of Jesus' garments among his executioners.[16] There is reason to believe that they could have made claim to his clothing, possibly, as the gospels note, by gambling to see who got what. Such a division could well be "history remembered." There is one caution: Psalm 22 was cited to aid early Christian understanding of Jesus' death. In that psalm we read:

> They divide my clothes among themselves,
> and for my clothing they cast lots. (v. 18; LXX v. 19)[17]

In John's gospel the reference is specific (19:24). Again, we may have an example of "prophecy historicized."

F. The Inscription

All the gospels record that the charge for which Jesus was condemned was written on some sort of sign either attached to the cross or displayed nearby.[18] The precise wording cannot be determined, but the import was that Jesus claimed to be "king of the Jews." This was the core of the interrogation before Pilate. The judgment of Brown is: "I see no convincing objection to its historicity as the expression of the charge on which the Romans executed Jesus."[19] The gospel record never denies the charge, but rather seeks to show it to be mistaken.

G. Those Crucified with Jesus

It is also the unanimous gospel testimony that two other criminals were crucified along with Jesus.[20] The familiar arrangement of one on either side of Jesus is also agreed upon in the gospel record. Multiple execution were common in the period. Just sixty years earlier six thousand rebel slaves had been crucified following the defeat of Spartacus. It would appear that Jesus was not alone on the crosses of Golgotha.

Yet, in affirming the historicity of a multiple execution we still acknowledge the possible influence of Isaiah's Suffering Servant passages.[21] In this instance, we have:

> Therefore I will allot him a portion with the great...
> because he poured out himself to death,
>   and was numbered with the transgressors. (53:12)

Nevertheless, "history remembered" rather than "prophecy historicized" appears the more likely source of the gospel record.

IV. JESUS ON THE CROSS

A. The Time and the Guard

In Mark's gospel we read: "It was nine o'clock in the morning when they crucified him" (15:25). However, in John's gospel Jesus is still in the presence of Pilate at noon (19:14). The two accounts cannot be reconciled. However, given the events of the day, Mark's timing seems the less likely.[22] It is more probable that Jesus was placed on the cross several hours prior to mid-afternoon.

An official guard was likely to have remained at the scene of the crucifixion, as Matthew specifies (27:36). Members of the guard also may have functioned as executioners, as John indicates (19:23). Brown affirms: "In the cast of characters involved in the gospel accounts, the most certain to have been there are the soldiers."[23] They will also serve the purposes of the evangelists. In the synoptics, from their number comes the centurion whose evaluation of the scene is crucial.[24] In Mark, the centurion testifies to the fact of Jesus' death (15:44–45). A soldier does the same in John (19:33–34).

B. The Mockery of Jesus

Given the public nature of the place of execution, the sufferings of the victims were usually augmented by the mockery of the passersby. We have no reason to doubt the synoptic accounts that Jesus was the object of such abuse. In Mark (who is followed by Matthew) the abuse is universal, including not only the passersby but also the enemies of Jesus and those crucified with him (15:29–45). "The presence [at the crucifixion] of some of the Sanhedrin members who had promoted Jesus' death is not at all implausible."[25] Luke numbers the soldiers— and one of the thieves crucified with him—among those who mock Jesus but has the "good thief" come to Jesus' defense (23:36, 40–41).[26]

Were there no friendly faces in the crowd? "The most difficult element to verify historically among the activities at the cross is the presence of friends of Jesus."[27] There may have been some of Jesus' entourage present.[28] However, the soldiers and the avowed enemies of Jesus certainly would have discouraged any supporters of Jesus from making their presence obvious. Still, it is possible that Jesus underwent his final hours abandoned by those who knew and loved him.[29]

C. The Last Words of Jesus

Nothing is quite as precious to the historian as the last words of the figure he is studying. Unfortunately, they are not often available. Frequently, traditions fill in the gap. Can we be sure that Caesar's last words were the famous "Et tu, Brute?" The expression deepens the Bard's theme of betrayal, which accounts for its presence.

It has been a time-honored custom to speak of "the seven last words of Jesus," giving the impression that these were uttered sequentially as Jesus hung on the cross. What appears more likely is that the evangelists each selected allusions to Old Testament passages that cast light on the meaning of Jesus' death. As the choices are different, we can assume that these final words of Jesus are "prophecy historicized," not "history remembered."

In Mark we have: "At three o'clock Jesus cried out with a loud voice, 'Eloi, Eloi, lema sabachthani?' which means, 'My God, my God, why have you forsaken me?'" (15:34). The quotation is an Aramaic version of the twenty-second psalm's opening line. Taken as a whole, the psalm is an expression of confidence in God during a time of great stress. The citation is in line with Mark's picture of a very human Jesus. Luke and John present quite different final words; in each case the choices reflect the author's theme. Much as we would like to do so in our search for the Jesus of history, it is probably not possible to determine what he might have said as his death approached.

V. THE DEATH OF JESUS

A. *He Breathes His Last*

The synoptics follow Mark's report: "When it was noon, darkness came over the whole land until three in the afternoon. At three o'clock Jesus cried out with a loud voice..." (15:33–34).[30] John does not cite a specific time, but mid-afternoon is not contradicted by his account (19:28–30). As for the gathering gloom, there are so many references in the Hebrew Bible to darkness as a sign from God that it is hard to reject the notion that what we have here is "prophecy historicized."[31]

At this juncture Mark, Matthew and John are in agreement that some-one offered Jesus a drink of vinegarized wine, apparently on sponge.[32] Luke places this occurrence earlier in his account (23:36). We noted above the possible reference to psalm 69:21. The scene is confused by the tradi-tion of an eschatological reference to the return of Elijah. Among the last lines in the Hebrew Bible's Book of the Prophets is Malachia's "I will send you the prophet Elijah before the great and terrible day of the LORD comes" (4:5; LXX 3:23). Behind what is "prophecy historicized" there also may have been someone who sought to ease Jesus' agony.

The synoptics also agree upon Jesus' final crying out in a loud voice. However, as we saw, neither the synoptics nor John are in agreement on the content of the final cry. Brown notes: "It is not inconceivable that his-torically a Jesus tortured by his sufferings gave voice to his desperation by using a psalm prayer describing the despondent condition of a suffering just one."[33] Perhaps, then, all we can say is that at the point of death Jesus did cry out.

The synoptics simply state that at the end Jesus "breathed his last."[34] John writes: "Then he bowed his head and gave up his spirit" (19:30), giving the impression that Jesus himself willed to die rather than having his dying as the effect of his sufferings, a view supported by the shortness of his time on the cross. There has been considerable speculation over the years as to the actual causes. Brown cites a study that reports: "Shock brought on by dehydration and loss of blood is the only plausible medical explanation for the death of the crucified Jesus."[35]

B. Reactions in the Synoptics

As Brown tells the reader: "It was widely understood in antiquity that God of the gods frequently gave extraordinary signs at the death of noble or important figures."[36] It is thus not surprising that the gospel traditions would record similarly extraordinary phenomena following the death of Jesus. Mark, followed by Matthew and Luke, reports that "the curtain of the temple was torn in two, from top to bottom" (15:38).[37] Matthew adds other phenomena to the scene (27:51–53). Having no outside evidence of these occurrences, we have to remain skeptical about their historicity.

We turn then to those cited as witnesses to Jesus' death. We have already noted the presence of soldiers at the cross. Following Mark, the synoptics single out one of these: "Now when the centurion, who stood facing him, saw that in this way he breathed his last, he said, 'Truly this man was God's Son!'" (15:39).[38] It certainly suits Mark's purpose to have a Roman soldier, especially a centurion, give testimony to Jesus as God's Son. It is also something no other human being does in the first of the gospels. In Luke, the centurion gives testimony to Jesus' innocence (23:47). Given the thematic role of the centurion, his historicity too must be doubted, though the presence of soldiers need not be.

The evangelists speak of a group of women present at the execution. In Mark, Matthew and John they are identified, though with some variation (Mk 15:40–41; Mt 27:55–56; Jn 19:25). These onlookers perform a crucial function in their respective gospels. They are witnesses to where Jesus was entombed: "Mary Magdalene and Mary the mother of

Joses saw where the body was laid" (Mk 15:47); "Mary Magdalene and the other Mary were there, sitting opposite the tomb" (Mt 27:61); "the women who had come with him from Galilee followed, and they saw the tomb and how his body was laid" (Lk 23:55). They and they alone bridge the gap between Friday evening and Sunday morning. Again, the thematic purpose casts doubt on their historicity.

C. The Johannine Reactions

John's gospel has the most elaborate scenario following Jesus' death:

> Since it was the day of Preparation, the Jews did not want the bodies left on the cross during the sabbath, especially because that sabbath was a day of great solemnity. So they asked Pilate to have the legs of the crucified men broken and the bodies removed. Then the soldiers came and broke the legs of the first and of the other who had been crucified with him. But when they came to Jesus and saw that he was already dead, they did not break his legs. Instead, one of the soldiers pierced his side with a spear, and at once blood and water came out. (19:31–34)

The gospel then indicates that the author was a witness to the scene. Brown suggests that

> there was behind the Johannine community and its traditions a disciple of Jesus, not a major figure by outside standards (e.g., not one of the Twelve) but one whose subsequent role in Johannine life showed that he was specially loved by Jesus.[39]

We cannot be sure that such a figure was in fact an eyewitness, though he certainly had a role in the formation of the Johannine traditions.

The view that John's account of Jesus' death is more "prophecy historicized" than "history remembered" is reinforced by the evangelist's citations: "These things occurred so that the scripture might be fulfilled, 'None of his bones shall be broken.' And again another passage of scripture says, 'They will look on the one whom they have pierced'" (19:36–37). Exodus is speaking of the Paschal lamb when it commands: "You shall not break any of its bones (12:46). Behind the other citation we have Zechariah:

And I will pour out a spirit of compassion and supplication on the house of David and the inhabitants of Jerusalem, so that, when they look on the one whom they have pierced, they shall mourn for him, as one mourns for an only child, and weep bitterly over him, as one weeps over a firstborn. (12:10)

VI. THE BURIAL OF JESUS

A. Was Jesus Buried?

As Crossan points out: "For the ancient world, the final penalty was to lie unburied as food for carrion birds and beasts."[40] In the same period as Jesus' life ended, there were prominent Romans who chose suicide rather than execution for treason because the former fate allowed one to be buried.[41] The presumption is that Jesus, executed under Roman law, would have been left hanging on the cross. Crossan gives the greater weight to this possibility.[42]

From the perspective of Roman law alone, Brown agrees with Crossan, noting that "little indeed would be the likelihood that the prefect of Judea would have given the body of this crucified would-be king to his followers for burial."[43] But what of the Jewish point of view? We read in the Book of Deuteronomy:

When someone is convicted of a crime punishable by death and is executed, and you hang him on a tree, his corpse must not remain all night upon the tree; you shall bury him that same day, for anyone hung on a tree is under God's curse. You must not defile the land that the LORD your God is giving you for possession. (21:22–23)

In the light of such a specific command, Brown concludes, "That Jesus was buried is historically certain."[44]

B. The Gospel Accounts

1. JOSEPH OF ARIMATHEA

All agree it was "the day of Preparation" preceding a sabbath. As we noted, in John's chronology the following Sabbath was also Passover. There is similar agreement that one Joseph of Arimathea went to Pilate and requested Jesus' body.[45] Mark describes him as "a respected member of the council." Matthew and John say that he was "a disciple of

Jesus," though John reports that due to fear he kept it a secret. Unfortunately, there is no agreement among scholars on the location of Arimathea, save that it was not in Galilee.

His request is granted making possible the burial of Jesus. Obviously the historicity of this Joseph of Arimathea is crucial. Brown concludes: "While high priority is not certitude, there is nothing in the basic preGospel account of Jesus' burial by Joseph that could not plausibly be deemed historical."[46] He sees it as unlikely that the Christian traditions would have created a sympathetic Jewish leader to carry out so essential a role.

The Marcan account of the burial is brief: "Then Joseph bought a linen cloth, and taking down the body, wrapped it in the linen cloth, and laid it in a tomb that had been hewn out of the rock. He then rolled a stone against the door of the tomb" (15:46). The other versions are in substantial agreement.[47] As Brown believes, the present site honored as that of the tomb of Jesus has considerable archeological support.[48]

2. THE OTHERS PRESENT AT THE BURIAL

We have already noted that in the synoptic account, several women witnessed the burial of Jesus. John does not mention these women; rather, he has Nicodemus assist Joseph is the burial itself (19:39–42).[49] There are a number of ways suggested to account for Nicodemus, who is mentioned only in the Fourth Gospel. Brown sums the matter up: "I see no reason for denying Nicodemus a possible historicity; but that judgement does not guarantee he had a role in the burial."[50]

Though they were not present at the burial itself, Matthew speaks of another group of witnesses:

> The next day, that is, after the day of Preparation, the chief priests and the Pharisees gathered before Pilate and said, "Sir, we remember what that impostor said while he was still alive, 'After three days I will rise again.' Therefore command the tomb to be made secure until the third day; otherwise his disciples may go and steal him away, and tell the people, 'He has been raised from the dead,' and the last deception would be worse than the first." Pilate said to them, "You have a guard of soldiers; go, make it as secure as you can." So they went with the guard and made the tomb secure by sealing the stone. (27:62–66)

The presence of the guard at the tomb, found only in Matthew, is obviously meant to refute the later explanation for the empty tomb—that it was found empty because Jesus' body was stolen by his disciples. As the gospel itself says, "This story is still told among the Jews to this day" (28:15). This apologetic purpose does not itself negate the possible historicity of the presence of a guard at the tomb. What does challenge their historicity is their absence in Mark, Luke and John. In fact, as we will see, if such a guard were present on Easter morn, the other accounts of what happened make no sense. Brown concludes, "There is neither internal nor external evidence to cause us to affirm historicity."[51]

Now, as the sun sets and the sabbath rest begins—a sabbath that in John is also the Passover—silence reigns. From among those unfortunates crucified on that day, one body is missing. It rests in a tomb nearby. For the believer, the world is at the point of transformation. Soon nothing will be the same.

Chapter Twelve

AFTERMATH

I. THE RESURRECTION

The earliest Christian document we have, Paul's first letter to the Thessalonians, has the Apostle complimenting the believers in Macedonia and Achaia:

> For the people of those regions report about us what kind of welcome we had among you, and how you turned to God from idols, to serve a living and true God, and to wait for his Son from heaven, whom he raised from the dead—Jesus, who rescues us from the wrath that is coming. (1:9–10)[1]

The central character of Paul's conviction is made clear: "If Christ has not been raised, then our proclamation has been in vain and your faith has been in vain" (1 Cor 15:14).

Yet, neither in the gospels nor in any other New Testament document is the actual resurrection of Jesus said to have been witnessed by someone. Our judgment on the historicity of the event rests on evaluating the reports of the "empty tomb" and the claims of those who saw Jesus after the event.

II. THE EMPTY TOMB

The basic synoptic account is in Mark:

> When the sabbath was over, Mary Magdalene, and Mary the mother of James, and Salome bought spices, so that they might go and anoint him. And very early on the first day of the week, when the sun had risen, they went to the tomb. They had been saying to one another, "Who will roll

away the stone for us from the entrance to the tomb?" When they looked up, they saw that the stone, which was very large, had already been rolled back. (16:1–4)

Matthew identifies the women as "Mary Magdalene and the other Mary" (28:1), and Luke refers to them as the "women who had come with [Jesus] from Galilee" (23:55). In John's account it is a solitary figure who comes to the tomb: "Early on the first day of the week, while it was still dark, Mary Magdalene came to the tomb and saw that the stone had been removed from the tomb" (20:1).

All of the women discover that Jesus' body is no longer where it had been buried. Instead they are greeted by an apparition, variously described in the synoptics as "a young man," "an angel of the Lord" and "two men." In John, Mary Magdalene is confronted by "two angels."[2] These figures tell of Jesus' resurrection, save in John where Mary Magdalene encounters Jesus himself.

In Matthew, Luke and John it is the women (or woman) who bring the news to the disciples.[3] In a culture where the role of women was denigrated, it is not likely that the Christian tradition would have invented such a crucial role for these women. In fact, there is indication of a certain reticence in doing so. Luke notes: "But these words seemed to [the apostles] an idle tale, and they did not believe them" (24:11). In John, Peter and another disciple, "the one whom Jesus loved," rush to verify Mary Magdalene's report (20:2–8).

The empty tomb was crucial evidence of Jesus' being raised from the dead. This can be seen in Matthew's passage about the guards placed at the tomb. The Jewish leadership bribe them to report falsely to Pilate: "You must say, 'His disciples came by night and stole him away while we were asleep.'" Matthew adds: "And this story is still told among the Jews to this day" (28:13, 15). Such a counter-apologetic indicates the existence of an early attempt to discredit the story of the empty tomb.

We come to the pertinent question: Did the reports of the empty tomb flow from the Christian belief in Jesus' resurrection or did they precede it? Did some women (and the testimony is uniform here) find the tomb empty and report the fact to Jesus' followers? Brown notes: "The most frequently cited argument still has force: How did the preaching that Jesus was victorious over death ever gain credence if his corpse or skeleton lay in a tomb known to all?"[4] Moreover, if the story were fashioned to support the belief, why entrust the discovery to women, whose reports would have less probative value than reports of men? All in all, the existence of the empty tomb cannot simply be dismissed as having no foundation in history.

III. THE POST-RESURRECTION APPEARANCES

Writing to the Corinthians, the Apostle Paul lists several post-resurrection appearances of Jesus:

> For I handed on to you as of first importance what I in turn had received: that Christ died for our sins in accordance with the scriptures, and that he was buried, and that he was raised on the third day in accordance with the scriptures, and that he appeared to Cephas, then to the twelve. Then he appeared to more than five hundred brothers and sisters at one time, most of whom are still alive, though some have died. Then he appeared to James, then to all the apostles. Last of all, as to one untimely born, he appeared also to me. (1 Cor 15:3–8)

The earliest of the gospels, in contrast, gives no account of any appearances of the risen Christ.[5] In Mark, the women who come to the tomb and find it empty are given a message: "But go, tell his disciples and Peter that he is going ahead of you to Galilee; there you will see him, just as he told you" (16:7). Matthew elaborates such a meeting in Galilee (28:16–20). Jesus concludes by promising to not to leave them: "And remember, I am with you always, to the end of the age" (28:20).

In Luke the appearances are more extensive. At the close of his gospel and at the beginning of the Book of Acts he has the risen Christ remain in the presence of his followers for forty days before ascending into the skies (Lk 24:36–51; Acts 1:4–9). John also records several encounters with the risen Jesus. The first is with Mary Magdalene, in which Jesus speaks of ascending (20:14–17). There follow the appearances to the assembled apostles in Jerusalem (20:19–30). In what seems an epilogue to the gospel, John records a final encounter; this time with seven of his followers on the shore of the Sea of Galilee.

We agree with Crossan when he observes:

Even a reader totally innocent of questions about source or genre notices a drastic change in moving from the passion and burial stories to the resurrection and apparition ones. More specifically, it is very simple to compose a single harmonized version of the former narratives up to the finding of the empty tomb but flatly impossible to compose one for the latter traditions.[6]

The primitive character of tradition that Jesus of Nazareth was raised from the dead cannot be denied. As Sanders affirms:

That Jesus' followers (and later Paul) had resurrection experiences is, in my judgement, a fact. What the reality was that gave rise to the experiences I do not know....The resurrection is not, strictly speaking, part of the story of the historical Jesus, but rather belongs to the aftermath of his life.[7]

Brown is in agreement: "Yet, even if by comparative exegesis we can trace this idea back to the earliest days, we cannot prove that this Christian understanding corresponded to what really happened. That is a matter of faith."[8]

The believer searching for the Jesus of history can go no further than the empty tomb. Beyond it lies the Jesus of faith and the history of those who shared that faith.

IV. THE FADED FRESCO

A. *The Nazorean*

We began our search with an important distinction in mind: "The historical Jesus is not the real Jesus. The real Jesus is not the historical Jesus."[9] That "real Jesus" is the person who lived and died some two thousand years ago. We knew the results of our efforts would be limited: "Of its very nature, this quest can reconstruct only fragments of a mosaic, the faint outline of a faded fresco."[10] Yet our search may have given us a Jesus of history that is less of a "faded fresco."

For one thing, we should no longer see Jesus of Nazareth as the sole child in that trio called the Holy Family. Whatever weight we give to the Marcan view of Jesus as one in a bustling family of siblings, we should always see him in the midst of an extended group of assorted relatives with "cousins by the dozens," all bound together by the interdependence that still characterizes village life. It should be remembered that from childhood to maturity Jesus was so much the Nazorean that those who shared that life with him could not accept him as something more than the fellow villager they had known (Mk 6:2–3).

He was a rural villager, a Galilean. His accent would have betrayed him. His stories, his imagery, were drawn from the life that he knew for some thirty years. His urban opponents may have thought his simplicity to be ignorance. That often happens. In the case of Jesus, it was a wisdom gained from his roots in his experiences as a Nazorean, an artisan, a family man.

B. The Jew

Jesus was a Jew, a Jew by culture and by religion. He certainly inherited and observed the traditions of his people. As a child he would have heard all the stories that enrich those traditions. We may discount the accuracy of the "genealogies" of Matthew (1:1–16) and of Luke (3:23–38), but we need not doubt that Jesus himself accepted the great figures of Israel's history as his own ancestors. In the early years of Christianity there was an understandable tendency to mitigate that Jewishness, but we should never lose sight of it.

Nor should we fail to take into account the depth of religious life in a village such as Nazareth. It may not have been as strictly observant as the Pharisees would have liked, but it was a powerful component of Jesus' environment. From the moment of his circumcision, Jesus became not only one with his people but began his participation in their age-old ritual life. The Jesus who frequented the synagogues in his public ministry certainly was no less faithful in his earlier years.[11] Similarly, with family and friends he would have made yearly pilgrimages to Jerusalem. It was an involvement that continued until the very night before he died. Christianity's own profound relationship with Judaism has its roots in the formative years of Jesus, the Jew from Nazareth.

C. The Impact of John the Baptizer

Often we cannot easily determine what causes the dramatic changes in a person's life. Whatever it was in Jesus' case, one crucial aspect was his encounter with John the Baptizer. Famous, persuasive, ascetic, destined for a martyr's fate, John may have for a time enlisted Jesus as a follower.

The impact was impressive. It changed the life of the Nazorean. To appreciate the transformation we have to see the change against normalcy of his life as a Galilean villager. At thirty or so Jesus was most likely the head of an extended family, a craftsman and certainly a pillar of the life in his village.[12] Then, in a manner that left his family, friends and fellow Nazoreans puzzled at best, all that changed radically.

D. The Ministry of Jesus

Save for the single visit mentioned in the synoptic gospels, Jesus did not go home again after his encounter with John. Capernaum is now spoken of as his home (Mk 2:1), but most of his time is spent literally "on the road." I have described him as a charismatic sage, moving about dispensing wise advice and religious guidance, usually in the form of stories or parables. He also gains a reputation as a healer. The pattern was that of a Hasid, a holy man who had counterparts in the Palestine of that period.

Around him gathered a group of followers, some inherited from the Baptizer. There were both men and women; the latter may have provided the necessary financial support (Mk 15:40–41) as they moved from village to village. Though usually traveling in lower Galilee, he did visit surrounding areas. Jesus spoke in the synagogues, town squares, on the shores of the lake, at crossroads, wherever a crowd, large or small, could be gathered. His ministry lasted an estimated two to two-and-a-half years.

Jesus drew on his own experiences, experiences he shared with his followers and hearers. His message reflected what it was to be a pious Jew in a rural village. Perhaps it is here that the first hint of trouble arises. His initial clashes were with the Pharisees, a "law and order" group with little sympathy for a free-lance Hasid who gave cavalier interpretations of the Law. Word of him soon reached Jerusalem with its great Temple. There the leaders were sensitive to any challenge, especially if that challenge threatened their relationship with Rome. They apparently sent representatives to investigate one who might become a danger (Mk 3:22; 7:1).

E. The Apocalyptic

It is an assumption, but it is possible that Jesus' message changed its emphasis. As the clouds darkened, Jesus seems to have shifted his focus to an impending cataclysm that would mark the establishment of God's kingdom on earth. There was an increasing urgency to his message. It became apocalyptic in tone. He spoke of those who would survive and those who would perish. It was increasingly a call for prompt decision. Unfortunately, such language could only further alienate those who were already suspicious of him.

The threat grew when his followers spoke of Jesus as being another of the prophets or the expected Messiah, titles that would only serve to increase the alarm of the Jewish leadership. Still more disturbing would have been hints of Jesus' own role in the coming of the kingdom. Any hint of being a royal claimant would have alerted Palestine's Roman overlords.

F. The Challenge

Perhaps had Jesus remained in lower Galilee things would have gone no further, but his mission inevitably took him to Jerusalem, certainly more than once. Moreover, at either the beginning, as indicated in John, or at the end of his ministry, as in the synoptics, Jesus made a dramatic gesture of disapproval by driving the merchants and moneychangers from the Temple precincts. Such a prophetlike challenge to the very center of Judaism could hardly have gone without a response from the authorities.

For a final time Jesus came the Holy City for the celebration of Passover. His notoriety was such that some demonstration occurred upon his entrance to the city. Later there were confrontations between Jesus and his critics in the Temple precincts. For a time Jesus' popularity and the Jewish leadership's fear of a disturbance served to protect Jesus. Then his enemies were presented with an unexpected opportunity: one of Jesus' own followers was willing to betray him into their hands.

Jesus himself was not oblivious to the threat; indeed, he appears to be aware that events are coming to a head. Though easily able to do so, he makes no effort to avoid disaster. In fact, he seems to regard his own fate as essential to the completion of his mission. At a meal, remembered as the last one he shared with followers, Jesus added words of interpretation to the ritual blessings of the food. These words were meant to prepare his companions for what he thought was inevitable. Jesus believed his death would be the sacrifice that would initiate God's climatic act of salvation.

G. *Betrayal, Trial and Condemnation*

Possibly that very same night Jesus and his immediate followers retired to an olive grove outside the city, taking refuge in a cave. It was Judas's foreknowledge of this that provided the opportunity for his betrayal. With a force provided by the Judean leadership, Jesus was seized. Though some may have sought to defend Jesus at first, in the end his companions deserted him en masse.

What happened next bears out the report of Josephus: "Pilate, because of an accusation made by leading men among us, condemned him to the cross." Jesus was taken before the high priest and his advisors. He was interrogated, ostensibly to determine his guilt. But the interrogation was a mockery because the leadership had already determined to do away with him. The charge was to be blasphemy, a capital crime, but they were not going to do the dirty work themselves. Jesus was turned over to the Roman procurator.

From what history tells us of Pontius Pilate, we can assume he would deal decisively and harshly with any threat to the public order. If Jesus was presented to him as someone laying claim to an ancient regal line of Israel and attracting crowds in the process, the outcome would be a foregone conclusion. At the time it was probably a routine condemnation, of little significance except to a few of those involved. Charged with sedition, Jesus was led off to be crucified after first being flogged. Apparently he was so weakened at this point that a bystander was forced to carry the crossbeam usually carried by the victim himself.

H. *Death by Crucifixion*

The gospel accounts spare us the details of what was a particularly horrible and degrading form of execution. Flanked by two other unfortunates, Jesus was nailed to a crossbeam and hoisted onto an upright post to which his feet were attached. There he hung for some three hours, undergoing the mockery of guards, his enemies and passersby. If we follow the Fourth Gospel's chronology, it was the Preparation day for Passover. Jesus dies at the time when the lambs to be used in the ritual meal were being sacrificed in the Temple.

The fact that the following day was the great feast may have motivated a Jew of some influence to petition Pilate for the body so that it could be removed and buried before sunset. The request was granted. As there were tombs in the immediate area of the site of the execution, Jesus was laid to rest in one of them. On the first day of the following week the tomb was found to be empty. Our "faded fresco" is complete.

V. FROM HISTORY TO CHURCH

Why did the execution of a possible revolutionary, active at the edge of the empire, come to the attention of a Jewish and two Roman historians (Josephus, Tacitus and Suetonius) by the end of the first century C.E.? The answer is simple. Very shortly after Jesus' execution and burial a number of his followers insisted that he had been resurrected.[13] In time, others, Jews and Gentiles, came to share that conviction. Nor was it long before groups identified as Christians appeared in other cities of the empire. We have the report of Suetonius that well within a generation these Christians were present in Rome in sufficient number to cause serious disturbances among the city's Jewish population. Soon these Christian groups are being referred to as "churches" (1 Thes 1:1, 2:14). Finally, "*the* church" appears, embracing all those who accept Jesus as the Christ, the Messiah.

Luke Timothy Johnson states in *The Real Jesus:*

> I will argue that Christian faith has never—either at the start or now—been *based on historical reconstructions of Jesus,* even though Christian faith has always involved some historical claims concerning Jesus.[14]

Our "faded fresco" is not the "real" Jesus. Still, the "real" Jesus lies behind the "faded fresco." No matter how incomplete and even debatable it may be, the Jesus of history is our assurance that the "real" Jesus is anchored in history. He is no myth. It is also that "faded fresco" that brings home to us an essential truth. In the letter to the Hebrews, the author, speaking of Jesus, reminds us: "For we do not have a high priest who is unable to sympathize with our weaknesses, but we have one who in every respect has been tested as we are, yet without sin" (4:15).

It is important that we never lose sight of Jesus, the Nazorean villager, the Galilean Hasid, the one who knew family life with all of its ups and downs, knew what it meant to walk the roads of Palestine, here rejected, there accepted. He experienced warm friendship and cruel betrayal. Events shook him as events shake us. Yes, he was afraid. But he conquered fear. Only if we have such a Jesus of history will the "real" Jesus be more to us than myth.

NOTES

FOREWORD

1. As early as the mid-second century there were attempts to produce a single "biography" of Jesus drawn from the four gospel accounts.

2. Notable filmmakers have consistently presented "biographies" of Jesus. This would be true of the classic *The King of Kings* by Cecil B. De Mille (1937), as well as *The Gospel According to Matthew* by the Italian Pier Pasolini (1964) and *The Greatest Story Ever Told* by George Stevens (1965). Even Martin Scorsese's radically different depiction of Jesus in *The Last Temptation of Christ* still has a "biographical" form.

3. I will follow the contemporary custom of using C.E. (common era) and B.C.E. (before the common era) for A.D. and B.C.

4. *New Jerome Biblical Commentary,* ed. Raymond E. Brown, Joseph A. Fitzmyer, Roland E. Murphy (Englewood Cliffs, N.J.: Prentice-Hall, 1990). Subsequently referred to as *NJBC.*

5. *NJBC,* 1142b.

6. I prefer to use *Hebrew Bible* rather than *Old Testament.*

7. The term *church* in scripture may refer to an individual community of Christians, the Christian communities of a locality or Christianity as a whole.

8. Two volumes have already appeared and a third is projected.

9. In 1994 Crossan published a "distillation" of this work under the title *Jesus: A Revolutionary Biography.* Then, in 1995, he produced *Who Killed Jesus?*, a response to Brown's work of the previous year.

10. This is a two-volume work and, at the same time, Father Brown re-edited his monumental *The Birth of the Messiah.*

INTRODUCTION

1. Recently, the historian Garry Wills was awarded a Pulitzer prize for his new insights into the Gettysburg Address, certainly a previously well-studied document of Lincolniana.

2. John P. Meier, *A Marginal Jew: Rethinking the Historical Jesus* (New York: Doubleday, 1991), 1:21.

3. The area gets its name from the Philistines, who were its occupants at the time of the Jewish conquest of the "promised land."

4. Meier, *A Marginal Jew*, 1:197.

5. Ibid.

6. Luke Timothy Johnson, *The Real Jesus,* Harper San Francisco: 1996), 133.

7. This process, referred to as the development of doctrine, has been much debated but is now generally accepted by Catholic theologians.

8. Meier, *A Marginal Jew,* 1:25.

9. Ibid., 1:199.

10. Ibid.

11. We can see this by contrasting crucifixes that show a Jesus almost without flaw with those that depict Jesus as a mass of gaping wounds.

12. Meier, *A Marginal Jew*, 1:199.

13. Ibid.

14. Ibid.

CHAPTER ONE: THE SOURCES

1. Josephus, *Jewish Antiquities* 20.9.1.

2. Ibid., 18.3.3.

3. Tacitus, Cornelius, *The Annals of Imperial Rome*, trans. with an intro. by Michael Grant, rev. ed. with new bibliography (Harmondsworth, England; New York, N.Y.: Penguin Books, 1971), 365.

4. Suetonius (Gaius Suetonius Tranquillus), *The Twelve Caesars,* trans. Robert Graves, rev. and intro. Michael Grant (London; New York: Penguin Books, 1989 [1979]), 202.

5. In the New Testament a series of letters are attributed to St. Paul. However, in the view of contemporary scripture scholarship, only 1 Thessalonians, Galatians, Philippians, 1 and 2 Corinthians, Romans and Philemon give evidence of having been written by the Apostle and thus are regarded as authentic.

6. According to Acts 11:26, the practice began in Antioch of Syria.

7. Rodney Stark, *The Rise of Christianity: A Sociologist Reconsiders History* (Princeton, N.J.: Princeton University Press, 1996).

8. Wayne A. Meeks, *The First Urban Christians: The Social World of the Apostle Paul* (New Haven: Yale University Press, 1983), 8.

9. Ibid., 29.

10. At root, *church* means an "assembly" or "congregation," not a building. A detailed discussion of the roles of the house churches and local churches can be found in Philip J. Cunningham, *Mark: The Good News Preached to the Romans* (Mahwah, N.J.: Paulist Press, 1995).

11. Eventually "bishop" was derived from the term. Other leaders were referred to as *presbyteroi,* the Greek for "elder."

12. At first these were on paper made from papyrus. Later animal skins (parchment) were used. Individual sheets were glued together to make scrolls.

13. From the Greek *kanon* meaning "rule."

14. Raymond Brown, "Canonicity," *New Jerome Biblical Commentary [NJBC],* ed. Raymond E. Brown, Joseph A. Fitzmyer, Roland E. Murphy (Englewood Cliffs, N.J.: Prentice-Hall, 1990), 1050.

15. "By the stricter standards current today, it may be legitimately questioned whether a single [New Testament] work comes directly from any one of the Twelve" (Brown, *NJBC,* 1044).

16. Ibid.

17. Ibid., 1051.

18. I prefer to date Mark as some time after 70 C.E., with Matthew and Luke appearing ten or fifteen years later (see Cunningham, *Mark: The Good News Preached to the Romans,* 13–16).

19. For a brief but excellent discussion of these early Christian communities, see Raymond Brown, *The Churches the Apostles Left Behind* (Mahwah, N.J.: Paulist Press, 1984).

20. For a readable, though partisan, view of this debate see Burton L. Mack, *The Lost Gospel: The Book of Q and Christian Origins* (Harper San Francisco, 1993).

21. For a detailed discussion of this see Raymond Brown, *The Community of the Beloved Disciple* (Mahwah, N.J.: Paulist Press, 1979).

22. An ancient group of Christians who resided in Egypt from the earliest days of the church.

23. Marvin Meyer, trans. and intro., *The Gospel of Thomas: The Hidden Sayings of Jesus* (Harper San Francisco, 1992), 10.

24. Pheme Perkins, "Apocrypha," *NJBC,* 1067.

25. For a detailed discussion of such a possibility, see Joachim Jeremias, *The Parables of Jesus*, rev. ed. (New York: Scribner's, 1963).

26. John P. Meier, *A Marginal Jew: Rethinking the Historical Jesus*, 2 vols. (New York: Doubleday, 1991), 1:68.

27. Norman Perrin, *Rediscovering the Teaching of Jesus* (New York: Harper & Row, 1976), 39.

28. Meier, *A Marginal Jew*, 1:172.

29. Ibid., 1:177.

30. John Dominic Crossan, *Who Killed Jesus? Exposing the Roots of Anti-Semitism in the Gospel Story of the Death of Jesus* (Harper San Francisco, 1995), 2–3.

31. Ibid., 1.

CHAPTER TWO: JESUS: A FIRST-CENTURY GALILEAN

1. In the sixth century an attempt was made to distinguish dates as "Before Christ" or in the "Year of the Lord" *(Anno Domini)*. Unfortunately, a four-year error was made in determining the date of Herod's death.

2. John P. Meier, *A Marginal Jew: Rethinking the Historical Jesus* (New York: Doubleday, 1991), 1:373.

3. Raymond E. Brown, *The Death of the Messiah: From Gethsemane to the Grave: A Commentary on the Passion Narratives in the Four Gospels* (New York: Doubleday, 1994), 1374.

4. After the reign of Solomon (960–925 B.C.E.), the country was divided between the north, called Israel, and the south, Judea.

5. It is the Hebrew word *Gilil* ("gentile") that lies behind the name of the area.

6. Geza Vermes, *Jesus the Jew: A Historian's Reading of the Gospels* (Philadelphia: Fortress Press, 1981 [1973]), 45.

7. Meier, *A Marginal Jew*, 1:282.

8. Ibid.

9. Ibid., 1:283.

10. Vermes, *Jesus the Jew*, 46.

11. Josephus, *The Jewish War*, trans. G. A. Williamson, rev. ed., with new introduction, notes and appendixes by E. Mary Smallwood (Harmondsworth, Middlesex, England; New York: Penguin, 1981, 1970), 133.

12. Vermes, *Jesus the Jew*, 47.

13. Ibid.

14. Meier, *A Marginal Jew,* 1:351.

15. E. P. Sanders, *The Historical Figure of Jesus* (London: Penguin Press, 1993), 12.

16. In Matthew's account Jesus' parents are Bethlamites who, on their return from Egypt, make Nazareth their home (Mt 2:22–23). In Luke, Jesus' parents are from Nazareth; they happen to be in Bethlehem when Jesus is born (Lk 2:4–6, 39).

17. Crossan, *Who Killed Jesus?* (Harper San Francisco, 1995), 15–16.

18. Meier, *A Marginal Jew*, 1:277.

19. Raymond E. Brown, *The Birth of the Messiah: A Commentary on the Infancy Narratives in Matthew and Luke* (Garden City, N.Y.: Doubleday, 1977), 33.

20. Ibid., 38.

21. The Greek word in question is *tekton,* and it has a broader meaning than "carpenter" (Meier, *A Marginal Jew*, 1:280–82).

22. John Dominic Crossan, *Jesus: A Revolutionary Biography* (Harper San Francisco, 1994), 25.

23. Meier, *A Marginal Jew*, 1:274.

24. Ibid., 275.

25. Learned in the Hebrew scriptures, these men were the intellectuals of Jewish society and often occupied positions of leadership.

26. Meier, *A Marginal Jew*, 278

27. Ibid., 1:331.

28. Some posit that the "brothers and sisters" were cousins. Other suggest that they might have been children of Joseph by an earlier marriage.

29. Meier, *A Marginal Jew*, 1:336.

30. C. H. Dodd, *The Parables of the Kingdom,* rev. ed. (New York, Scribner's, 1961), 20.

31. Joachim Jeremias, *The Parables of Jesus,* rev. ed. (New York, Scribner's, 1963).

32. A nuance is often overlooked. If just blown out, these oil lamps would smolder for hours. Putting them "under the bushel basket," that is, a container, is the best way of extinguishing such a lamp.

33. Unique to Luke, the reference to the nobleman in search of regal power may reflect the maneuvering of Archelaus, Herod the Great's son, to gain mastery over Judea as the common era began (Josephus *The Jewish War*, 120ff.).

CHAPTER THREE: JESUS THE JEW

1. In 587 B.C.E. the Babylonians destroyed Jerusalem and its Temple, leading many Jews off to exile in Babylon. When Cyrus, commanding the Persians and the Medes, conquered the Babylonians, he allowed the Jews to return home and begin the rebuilding of the city and the Temple (538 B.C.E.).

2. The Temple was never rebuilt. Jews still come to pray at its former site today.

3. Josephus, *The Jewish War*, trans. G. A. Williamson, rev. ed., with new introduction, notes and appendixes by E. Mary Smallwood (Harmondsworth, Middlesex, England; New York: Penguin, 1981, 1970), 133.

4. Tobit, Judith, 1–2 Maccabees, Wisdom, Sirach, Baruch and parts of Esther and Daniel found in the Septuagint were not accepted into the Hebrew canon.

5. We have the reference in Suetonius: "Since the Jews were constantly causing disturbances at the instigation of Chrestus, he [Claudius] expelled them from Rome" (Suetonius, [Gaius Suetonius Tranquillus], *The Twelve Caesars,* trans. Robert Graves, rev. and intro. Michael Grant [London; New York: Penguin Books, 1989 {1979}], 202). This was in 49 C.E.

6. Geza Vermes, *The Religion of Jesus the Jew* (Minneapolis: Fortress Press, 1993), 183.

7. Stephen M. Wylen, *The Jews in the Time of Jesus: An Introduction* (Mahwah, N.J.: Paulist Press, 1996), 87.

8. Ibid.

9. References to Jesus in the synagogues appear in Mk 1:39; 3:1; Mt 4:23; 9:35; 12:9; Lk 4:15, 33, 44; 6:6; 13:10; Jn 18:20.

10. For Nazareth, see Mk 1:21; Mt 13:54; Lk 4:16. For Capernaum, see Mk 1:21; Lk 4:38; Jn 6:59.

11. Wylen, *The Jews in the Time of Jesus*, 87.

12. Joachim Jeremias, *Jerusalem in the Time of Jesus: An Investigation into Economic and Social Conditions During the New Testament Period*, trans. F. H. and C. H. Cave (Philadelphia: Fortress Press, 1969), 29.

13. It is possible that this was the third of the Judaism's pilgrimage feasts, that of Weeks. It corresponded to what became later the Christian celebration of Pentecost. To avoid confusion John may have omitted mentioning the feast by name.

14. Vermes, *The Religion of Jesus the Jew*, 14.

15. Anthony J. Saldarini, "Apocrypha," in *New Jerome Biblical Commentary*, 1080.

16. E. P. Sanders, *The Historical Figure of Jesus* (London: Penguin Press, 1993), 43.

17. Mt 9:10–11; Lk 5:29–30; 7:34; 15:2.

18. Josephus, *The Jewish War,* 137.

19. Raymond E. Brown, *The Death of the Messiah: From Gethsemane to the Grave: A Commentary on the Passion Narratives in the Four Gospels* (New York: Doubleday, 1994), 356.

20. Jeremias *Jerusalem in the Time of Jesus*, 303–12.

21. Ibid.

CHAPTER FOUR: JESUS AND THE BAPTIZER

1. Josephus, *Jewish Antiquities*, quoted in John P. Meier, *A Marginal Jew: Rethinking the Historical Jesus* (New York: Doubleday, 1991), 2:20.

2. But not always. The four gospels also speak of one who "will baptize you with the Holy Spirit" (Mk 1:8; see also Jn 1:33). Jesus' sufferings also are spoken of as a "baptism" (Mk 10:38–39). *Q* speaks of a baptism in fire (Mt 3:11; Lk 3:16).

3. There is evidence that the Jewish "proselyte" baptism originated later in the first century C.E.

4. Meier, *A Marginal Jew*, 2:30.

5. Ibid.

6. Josephus, *Jewish Antiquities* 18.5.2, §§116, 118–19.

7. Meier, *A Marginal Jew*, 2:31. *Eschatological* is from the Greek *eskhatos,* meaning "last." Hence such a figure reveals what will happen at the end of time.

8. Ibid., 2:41.

9. Ibid., 2:101.

10. Ibid., 2:33.

11. Ibid., 2:35.

12. Ibid., 2:107.

13. Ibid., 2:120.

14. Ibid., 1: 129.

15. Ibid., 1:108–9.

CHAPTER FIVE: JESUS, THE CHARISMATIC SAGE

1. John P. Meier, *A Marginal Jew: Rethinking the Historical Jesus* (New York: Doubleday, 1991), 1:374.

2. Meier, *A Marginal Jew*, 1:382.

3. Ibid., 1:405.

4. Ibid., 1:237.

5. Burton L. Mack, *The Lost Gospel: The Book of Q and Christian Origins* (Harper San Francisco, 1993), 73–80.

6. Geza Vermes, *Jesus the Jew: A Historian's Reading of the Gospels* (Philadelphia: Fortress Press, 1981 [1973]), 58. Note Vermes's term *charismatic Judaism.* The word *charismatic* comes from the Greek *kharisma,* meaning "divine gift."

7. Ibid., 69.

8. Josephus in his *Jewish Antiquities* (14:22–24) also mentions Honi (*Onias* in the Greek). In the midst of a civil war between rival claimants to the Judean throne, one faction seized Honi and demanded that he call down God's curse on its rival. When he refused to do so, he was stoned to death. His captors did not doubt Honi's power to do what they demanded.

9. Gamaliel is mentioned in Acts (5:34) and is reported to have been the teacher of Paul (Acts 22:3).

10. Vermes, *Jesus the Jew*, 72.

11. In John 4:46 the person cured is the son of a royal official, not a centurian's slave.

12. Vermes, *Jesus the Jew*, 69, 79–80.

13. Ibid., 80.

14. Ibid., 81.

15. I do not want to overstate the case, however. As noted, Jesus lived almost in sight of the area's administrative center, Sepphoris. He is said to have visited Trye, Sidon, Caesarea Philippi, the territory of Gerasenes and the region of the Decapolis, all largely non-Jewish in character.

16. Vermes, *Jesus the Jew*, 81.

17. This is true, of course, if we discount the infancy narratives found in Matthew and Luke as historically inaccurate.

CHAPTER SIX: JESUS, THE MAN OF DEED

1. Geza Vermes, *Jesus the Jew: A Historian's Reading of the Gospels* (Philadelphia: Fortress Press, 1981 [1973]), 79.

2. Josephus, *Jewish Antiquities* 18.3.3.

3. "As a matter of empirical fact, an opinion survey published by George Gallup in 1989 found that about eighty-two percent of Americans polled believed that 'even today, miracles are performed by the power of God'" (John

P. Meier, *A Marginal Jew: Rethinking the Historical Jesus* [New York: Doubleday, 1991], 2:520).

4. John Dominic Crossan, *Jesus: A Revolutionary Biography* (Harper San Francisco, 1994), 82.

5. Unalterable "laws of nature" actually are more a concept of the nineteenth century than of modern science. Such concepts as quantum mechanics and the Heisenberg uncertainty principle have challenged the rigid predictability of earlier worldviews.

6. Meier, *A Marginal Jew*, 2:514–15.

7. Crossan, *Jesus*, 310.

8. Meier, *A Marginal Jew*, 2:535.

9. Ibid.

10. John L. McKenzie, S.J., *Dictionary of the Bible* (New York: Macmillan, 1965), 79a.

11. Vermes, *Jesus the Jew*, 69.

12. Suetonius (Gaius Suetonius Tranquillus), *The Twelve Caesars*, trans. Robert Graves, rev. with intro. by Michael Grant (London; New York: Penguin Books, 1989 [1979]), 284.

13. Phillip J. Cunningham, *Mark: The Good News Preached to the Romans* (Mahwah, N.J.: Paulist Press, 1995), 103–4. The scripture citations are: exorcising an unclean spirit: 1:23–26; restoring the sight of Bartimaeus: 10:46–52; curing fever, leprosy, and so on: 1:30–31; 1:40ff.; 2:3ff.; 3:1ff.; 5:25ff.; 7:32ff.; 8:22ff.; 10:46; 5:22ff.; 1:23–27; restoring a child to life: 5:2; driving out evil spirits: 7:26.

14. For these incidents, see Mk 4:37–39; 6:41; 6:48; 6:33–44; 8:1–9.

15. McKenzie, *Dictionary of the Bible*, 579b.

16. John speaks of the pool as having "five porticoes" (5:2), an unusual arrangement. However, just such a pool was discovered in Jerusalem, the fifth portico bisecting the pool. These incidents are reported in Jn 5:2–9; 6:1–12; 9:17; 11:1–44.

17. *Faith* is the customary New Testament translation of the Greek *pistis*. However, the word *trust* captures the Greek more fully.

18. The rather bizarre elements in the scene have led some to believe that it is a folktale incorporated into the gospel.

19. See Eph 6:16; 2 Thes 3:3; 1 Jn 2:13, 14; 3:12; 5:18–19; Mt 5:37; 6:13; 13:19, 38; Jn 17:15.

CHAPTER SEVEN: THE TITLES OF JESUS

1. Geza Vermes, *Jesus the Jew: A Historian's Reading of the Gospels* (Philadelphia: Fortress Press, 1981 [1973]), 86.

2. Ibid., 88.

3. John L. McKenzie, S.J., *Dictionary of the Bible* (New York: Macmillan, 1965), 694.

4. Vermes, *Jesus the Jew*, 94.

5. Ibid., 98.

6. Ibid., 99.

7. Ibid., 103.

8. Ibid., 121.

9. The title son of God appears, in one form or another, in Gal 2:20; 4:4, 6; 1 Cor 1:9; Rom 1:3–4, 9; 5:10; 8:3.

10. See also Jer 31:20; Hos 11:1; Dt 32:5–5, 18–19.

11. Vermes, *Jesus the Jew*, 209.

12. Ibid., 210.

13. John P. Meier, "Jesus," in *The New Jerome Biblical Commentary*, ed. Raymond E. Brown, Joseph A. Fitzmyer, and Roland E. Murphy, foreword by Carlo Maria Cardinal Martini (Englewood Cliffs, N.J.: Prentice-Hall, 1990), 1324.

14. The *NRSV*'s "I saw one like a human being" reflects the *meaning* of the text. The *New American Bible* translates the passage as: "I saw one like the son of man," reflecting the *language* of the text.

15. Vermes, *Jesus the Jew*, 185–86. The proposed solution is not without challenges, however. Cf. Meier, "Jesus," 1324–25.

16. Raymond E. Brown, *The Death of the Messiah: From Gethsemane to the Grave: A Commentary on the Passion Narratives in the Four Gospels* (New York: Doubleday, 1994), 1:515.

17. Vermes, *Jesus the Jew*, 134.

18. Ibid., 135.

19. The gospels of Matthew and Luke refer to Jesus as the son of David, stressing that Jesus was a descendant of the king. "The random use of title 'son of David' seems therefore to have no particular historical bearing. On the other hand, the phrase may have acted as a useful support in the early Christian argument concerning the Messiahship of Jesus" (Vermes, *Jesus the Jew*, 157).

20. Ibid., 129.

21. Brown, *The Death of the Messiah*, 1:480.

22. Vermes, *Jesus the Jew*, 156.

23. The understanding of Jesus' Divinity underwent a long period of devel-

opment, and there are variations in that understanding still. However, for any-one who believes Jesus to have been more than human, the challenge I mention exists.

24. In all of this discussion it must be kept in mind that it was not until the fourth century C.E. that the church in the first of the ecumenical councils defined with precision the person and nature of Jesus. Paul and other early church writers did not, could not, speak with such precision.

25. Philip J. Cunningham, *Mark: The Good News Preached to the Romans* (Mahwah, N.J.: Paulist Press, 1995), 91–96.

26. Ibid., 90.

CHAPTER EIGHT: JESUS AND THE KINGDOM OF GOD

1. John P. Meier, *A Marginal Jew: Rethinking the Historical Jesus* (New York: Doubleday, 1991), 2:237.

2. Ibid.

3. Geza Vermes, *The Religion of Jesus the Jew* (Minneapolis: Fortress Press, 1993), 121. "Kingdom" is used to translate the Greek *basileia*. Actually, "reign," "rule" or "kingly power" would be better because the term *kingdom* tends to have a geographical connotation that is not quite the biblical meaning. In the gospel of Matthew the parallel phrase is "kingdom of heaven." In using the circumlocution the evangelist most likely reflects the Jewish aversion to pronouncing the name of the Deity. The meaning, however, is the same.

4. Meier, *A Marginal Jew*, 2:239.

5. Ibid., 2:238. The pseudepigrapha are ancient documents that some claimed were part of Divine revelation, but they were never officially accepted as such (cf. John L. McKenzie, S.J., *Dictionary of the Bible* [New York: Macmillan, 1965], 42f.).

6. Ibid., 2:239.

7. Ibid., 2:270.

8. See also Pss 93:1–2; 96:10; 97:1; 145:11–13.

9. The Book of the Prophet Isaiah contains material written by three authors: the earliest wrote prior to the Exile, the second during the Exile and the last after the Exile.

10. See Is 41:21; 44:6; 52:7.

11. See Jer 8:19; 10:7, 10.

12. Meier, *A Marginal Jew*, 2:252.

13. Ibid., 2:289.

14. Ibid.

15. Vermes, *The Religion of Jesus the Jew*, 178.
16. Meier, *A Marginal Jew*, 2:299.
17. Ibid., 2:323, 325.
18. Ibid., 2:331
19. C. H. Dodd, *The Parables of the Kingdom,* rev. ed. (New York, Scribner, 1961), 13.
20. Meier, *A Marginal Jew*, 2:339–347.
21. Ibid., 2:423.
22. Ibid., 2:404.
23. Ibid., 2:31.

CHAPTER NINE: THE BEGINNING OF THE END

1. In 14:1 Mark combines two ancient Jewish festivals. One celebrated the spring harvest by the eating of unleavened bread. The other recalled the escape from slavery in Egypt under Moses by joining in the Passover meal (Seder).

2. Luke inserts an appearance of Jesus before Herod Antipas (23: 6ff.) and both Luke and Matthew place Jesus' crucifixion nearer noon, rather than at 9 A.M., as in Mark.

3. Between John and the synoptics there is a major conflict. The latter place the death of Jesus on the afternoon of the Passover. John is quite clear that the event took place on the day before.

4. Matthew 2:21 misunderstands the prophet's "riding on a donkey, on a colt, the foal of a donkey," thinking he is describing two animals rather than one, and thus he has Jesus strangely mounted.

5. Roland de Vaux, *Ancient Israel: Its Life and Institutions*, (New York, McGraw-Hill, 1961), 495. The others were the feasts of Passover and Weeks (Pentecost).

6. Ibid., 498.

7. This event is recorded in all four gospels. See Mk 11:15–19; Mt 21:10–17; Lk 19:45–48; Jn 2:13–16.

8. The synoptics place it on the first day of Holy Week (Matthew) or the second (Mark, Luke). In John, the event begins Jesus' public ministry.

9. Raymond E. Brown, *The Death of the Messiah: From Gethsemane to the Grave: A Commentary on the Passion Narratives in the Four Gospels* (New York: Doubleday, 1994), 144.

10. Joachim Jeremias, *The Eucharistic Words of Jesus* (Philadelphia:

Fortress Press, 1966), 189. In this and the following quotations from Jeremias, the emphases are his.

11. Ibid., 192.

12. John P. Meier, *A Marginal Jew: Rethinking the Historical Jesus* (New York: Doubleday, 1991), 302.

13. Jeremias, *The Eucharistic Words of Jesus*, 26.

14. Ibid., 42–62.

15. Though the olive grove was outside the city walls, it was still regarded as being within the city limits (cf. Jeremias, *The Eucharistic Words of Jesus*, 55).

16. See 1 Cor 11:23; Jn 13:30; Mk 14:17; Mt 26:20.

17. See Mk 14:18; Mt 26:20; Lk 22:14; Jn 13:12, 23, 25, 28. The *NRSV* uses the phrase "taking one's place" rather than "reclining."

18. For the synoptic accounts of the Last Supper details that follow, see Mk 14:22; Mt 26:26; Lk 22:19.

19. Jeremias, *The Eucharistic Words of Jesus*, 55.

20. Ibid., 56.

21. Ibid.

22. Ibid., 62.

23. See 1 Cor 5:7; 1 Pt 1:19; Rv 5:6, 9, 12; 12:11; Jn 1:29, 36.

24. Jeremias, *The Eucharistic Words of Jesus*, 82–83.

25. The story of the first Passover is recounted and the elements that make up the feast are explained.

26. The recitation of selections from Psalms.

27. Jeremias, *The Eucharistic Words of Jesus*, 85–86.

28. In the other accounts, Paul's (1 Cor 11:23–25), Mark's (14:22–25) and Matthew's (26:26–29), there are minor variations reflecting different ritual traditions.

29. Jeremias, *The Eucharistic Words of Jesus*, 88.

30. Ibid., 212.

31. Ibid., 217.

32. Ibid., 216.

33. Ibid., 109.

34. Again, all four gospels mention this. See Mk 14:17–21; Mt 26:20–25; Lk 22:21–23; Jn 13:26–30.

35. Jeremias, *The Eucharistic Words of Jesus*, 219.

36. Ibid., 221, 224.

37. Ibid., 225. The resurrection of Jesus became the cornerstone of the Christian faith at the earliest level. How clearly Jesus envisioned his own

future in those terms cannot be determined, save to say that he, without question, trusted in God to rescue him.

38. John concludes the Last Supper with, "After Jesus had spoken these words, he went out with his disciples across the Kidron" (18:1). That would be to go in the same direction as the Mount of Olives.

CHAPTER TEN: ARREST AND INTERROGATION

1. Raymond E. Brown, *The Death of the Messiah: From Gethsemane to the Grave: A Commentary on the Passion Narratives in the Four Gospels* (New York: Doubleday, 1994), 37.

2. Luke is unique in having Pilate send Jesus to Herod (23:6–16).

3. Brown, *The Death of the Messiah*, 148.

4. Ibid., 225–26.

5. Mk 14:36; Mt 26:39; Lk 22:42–44. The late-first-century letter to the Hebrews also makes reference to such a prayer: "In the days of his flesh, Jesus offered up prayers and supplications, with loud cries and tears, to the one who was able to save him from death, and he was heard because of his reverent submission" (5:7).

6. The accounts are found in Mk 14:43; Mt 26:47; Lk 22:47; Jn 18:3.

7. Brown, *The Death of the Messiah*, 263.

8. Cf. Mt 26:56. Mark then adds: "A certain young man was following him, wearing nothing but a linen cloth. They caught hold of him, but he left the linen cloth and ran off naked" (14:51–52.) Some have held that this was Mark himself. However, it is more likely that the author is simply showing the panic with which the followers of Jesus sought to escape.

9. Brown, *The Death of the Messiah*, 309.

10. *Synedrion* in Greek, which the *NRSV* translates "council."

11. Brown, *The Death of the Messiah*, 343.

12. John has an appearance of Jesus before Annas, father-in-law of Caiaphas, prior to Jesus meeting with the latter (18:13).

13. Brown, *The Death of the Messiah*, 426.

14. Ibid., 351, 362.

15. Mk 14:61; Mt 26:63; Lk 22:67, 70. The question is asked earlier in John (see 10:24).

16. Mk 14:63; Mt 26:65–66; Lk 22:71. John hints at such an accusation (see 10:36).

17. Brown, *The Death of the Messiah*, 476, 480, 478.

18. Ibid., 535.

19. Ibid.
20. Ibid., 536.
21. Ibid., 538.
22. Cf. Mt 26:61. John (2:19) connects the statement with Jesus' cleansing of the Temple at the beginning of his ministry (2:19).
23. Brown, *The Death of the Messiah*, 458.
24. Ibid., 546.
25. Ibid., 547.
26. Ibid., 586.
27. Peter's denial is referenced in Mk 14:54, 66–72; Mt 26:58, 69–75; Lk 22:54–62; Jn 18:15–18, 25–27.
28. Brown, *The Death of the Messiah*, 615.
29. At this juncture Matthew reports the violent death of Judas (27:3–10). Acts has a variant version (1:16–20). Here we have more of "prophecy historicized" that "history remembered," though some of the latter may remain.
30. Mk 15:1; Mt 27:1–2; Lk 23:1; Jn 18:28.
31. Josephus, *The Jewish War*, trans. G. A. Williamson, rev. ed., with new introduction, notes and appendixes by E. Mary Smallwood (Harmondsworth, Middlesex, England; New York: Penguin, 1981, 1970), 361–62.
32. Brown, *The Death of the Messiah*, 371.
33. Philo the Jew was an early-first-century C.E. Jewish author.
34. Brown, *The Death of the Messiah*, 704.
35. I have omitted Jesus' appearance before Herod (Luke 23:6–16). As Brown observes: "He [Luke] transmits a early tradition about Herod Antipas—tradition that had a historical nucleus but had already developed beyond simple history by the time it reached Luke" (*The Death of the Messiah*, 785). Recovery of that nucleus is not now possible.
36. Mk 15:2; Mt 27:11; Lk 23:3; Jn 18:33–37.
37. Brown, *The Death of the Messiah*, 731.
38. See Mk 15:2–5; Mt 27:11–14; Lk 23:2–5; Jn 18:28–38.
39. See Mk 15:14; Mt 27:23; Lk 23:22; Jn 19:12.
40. See Brown, *The Death of the Messiah*, 701–2.
41. Ibid., 813–14.
42. Ibid., 697.

CHAPTER ELEVEN: THE DEATH OF JESUS

1. Joseph, *Jewish Antiquities* 18.3.3.
2. Tacitus, Cornelius, *The Annals of Imperial Rome*, trans. and intro.

Michael Grant, rev. ed. with new bibliography (Harmondsworth, England; New York, N.Y.: Penguin Books, 1971), 15.44.

3. John Dominic Crossan, *Who Killed Jesus?: Exposing the Roots of Antisemitism in the Gospel Story of the Death of Jesus* (Harper San Francisco, 1995), 159.

4. Raymond E. Brown, *The Death of the Messiah: From Gethsemane to the Grave: A Commentary on the Passion Narratives in the Four Gospels* (New York: Doubleday, 1994), 14. By "earwitnesses" Brown means those who heard of the circumstances of Jesus' death and burial.

5. Ibid., 14, 51.

6. Ibid., 22.

7. Ibid., 53.

8. Was there a "pre-Marcan passion narrative" on which Mark depended? Brown states the current scholarship is evenly divided. If there was, he does not believe such a narrative can be reconstructed (Ibid., 54–55).

9. Ibid., 877.

10. Mk 15:21; Mt 27:32; Lk 23:26. John states clearly that Jesus was "carrying the cross by himself" (19:17). John tends to avoid giving the impression of any human weakness or limitation in his portrayal of Jesus.

11. Brown, *The Death of the Messiah*, 915.

12. This is the "Garden" Gate. The Church of the Holy Sepulchre in Jerusalem encloses the site today, and there is archeological evidence supporting the configuration of the area as described.

13. See Mk 15:24; Mt 27:35; Lk 23:33; Jn 19:18.

14. Josephus, Flavius, *The Jewish War*, trans. G. A. Williamson, rev. ed., with new introduction, notes and appendixes by E. Mary Smallwood (Harmondsworth, Middlesex, England; New York: Penguin, 1981, 1970), 390.

15. Brown, *The Death of the Messiah*, 949.

16. See Mk 15:24; Mt 27:35; Lk 23:34; Jn 19:23–24.

17. "LXX" stands for the "Septuagint" and is used to indicate when *NRSV* differs from the versification of the earlier version.

18. See Mk 15:26; Mt 27:37; Lk 23:38; Jn 19:19–22.

19. Brown, *The Death of the Messiah*, 968.

20. See Mk 15:27; Mt 27:37; Lk 23:33; Jn 19:18.

21. The passages are Isaiah 42:1–4; 49:1–6; 50:4–9; and 52:13–53:12.

22. Brown, *The Death of the Messiah*, 960.

23. Ibid., 1027.

24. See Mk 15:39; Mt 27:54; Lk 23:47.

25. Brown, *The Death of the Messiah,* 1027.

26. Jesus is not mocked in John's gospel, reflecting the theme of a divine-like Christ figure.

27. Brown, *The Death of the Messiah,* 1028.

28. See Mk 15:41; Mt 27:55; Lk 23:27; Jn 19:25 .

29. John's familiar scene of Jesus dying flanked by "the disciple Jesus loved" and his mother is dictated by the gospel's theme of a Jesus triumphant even in death.

30. Cf. Mt 27:45–46; Lk 23:44, 46.

31. Cf. Gn 1:2–3; Ex 10:21–23; Jer 15:9; Wis 5:6; Zeph 1:15; Jl 2:2, 10, 31; Am 8:9–10.

32. See Mk 15:36; Mt 27:48; Jn 19:29.

33. Brown, *The Death of the Messiah,* 1085.

34. See Mk 15:37; Mt 27:50; Lk 23:46.

35. Brown, *The Death of the Messiah,* 1092.

36. Ibid., 1113.

37. Cf. Mt 27:51; Lk 23:45. Josephus reports that veils from the Temple were carried through Rome as part of Titus's triumph after 70 C.E.. Members of Mark's community, living in Rome, could have seen these relics of the Temple's fate.

38. Cf. Mt 27:54; Lk 23:47.

39. Brown, *The Death of the Messiah,* 1193.

40. Crossan, *Who Killed Jesus?,* 160.

41. Tacitus, *The Annals of Imperial Rome,* vi, 29.

42. Crossan, *Who Killed Jesus?,* 187.

43. Brown, *The Death of the Messiah,* 1208.

44. Ibid., 1240.

45. See Mk 15:42–43; Mt 27:57–62; Lk 23:54–57; Jn 19:38.

46. Brown, *The Death of the Messiah,* 1241.

47. Mt 27:59–60; Lk 23:53; Jn 19:40–41.

48. Brown, *The Death of the Messiah,* 1279–83.

49. For Nicodemus himself, see Jn 3:1ff; 7:50–52.

50. Brown, *The Death of the Messiah,* 1279.

51. Ibid., 1312.

CHAPTER TWELVE: THE AFTERMATH

1. See also 1 Cor 6:14; Gal 1:1.

2. Mk 16:5; Mt 28:2; Lk 24:4; Jn 20:12.

3. Mt 28:8; Lk 24:8; Jn 20:2. It is generally agreed that Mark's gospel

ends: "So [the women] went out and fled from the tomb, for terror and amazement had seized them; and they said nothing to anyone, for they were afraid" (16:8). The additional verses (16:9–20) were added at a later date.

4. Raymond E. Brown, *The Gospel According to John* (Garden City, N.Y.: Doubleday, 1966–70), 1970, 976.

5. As I explained in *Mark: The Good News Preached to the Romans* (Mahwah, N.J.: Paulist Press, 1995) the author and his community were expecting the proximate return of the "risen" Christ who would bring history to a close. References to interim appearances would have been anti-climatic (see pp. 55–56).

6. John Dominic Crossan, *The Historical Jesus: The Life of a Mediterranean Jewish Peasant* (Harper San Francisco, 1991), 395.

7. E. P. Sanders, *The Historical Figure of Jesus* (London: Penguin Press, 1993), 276, 280.

8. Brown, *The Gospel According to John*, 967

9. John P. Meier, *A Marginal Jew: Rethinking the Historical Jesus* (New York: Doubleday, 1991), 1:21.

10. Ibid., 25.

11. It is true that no trace of an actual synagogue is found in ancient Nazareth. However, an open space or a private dwelling would have sufficed.

12. I recently heard Jesus referred to as a "young adult" at the time of his baptism by John. At a period in history when the average life-span was forty years, Jesus was fully mature.

13. There is no indication that his followers believed Jesus had been *resuscitated*. They experienced him as present to them in a special state referred to as his being "raised."

14. Luke Timothy Johnson, *The Real Jesus: The Misguided Quest for the Historical Jesus and the Truth of the Traditional Gospels* (Harper San Francisco, 1996), 133.

BIBLIOGRAPHY

Brown, Raymond E. *The Gospel According to John*. Garden City, N.Y.: Doubleday, 1966–70.

————. *The Birth of the Messiah: A Commentary on the Infancy Narratives in Matthew and Luke*. Garden City, N.Y.: Doubleday, 1977.

————. *The Community of the Beloved Disciple*. Mahwah, N.J.: Paulist Press, 1979.

————. *The Churches the Apostles Left Behind*. Mahwah, N.J.: Paulist Press, 1984.

————. "Canonicity." In *New Jerome Biblical Commentary*.

————. *The Death of the Messiah: From Gethsemane to the Grave: A Commentary on the Passion Narratives in the Four Gospels*. New York: Doubleday, 1994.

Cameron, Ron, ed. *The Other Gospels: Non-canonical Gospel Texts*. Philadelphia: Westminster Press, 1982.

Crossan, John Dominic. *The Historical Jesus: The Life of a Mediterranean Jewish Peasant*. Harper San Francisco, 1991.

————. *Jesus: A Revolutionary Biography*. Harper San Francisco, 1994.

————. *Who Killed Jesus? Exposing the Roots of Anti-Semitism in the Gospel Story of the Death of Jesus*. Harper San Francisco, 1995.

Cunningham, Phillip J., C.S.P. *Exploring Scripture: How the Bible Came to Be*. Mahwah, N.J.: Paulist Press, 1992.

————. *Mark: The Good News Preached to the Romans*. Mahwah, N.J.: Paulist Press, 1995.

Dodd, C. H. *The Parables of the Kingdom*. Rev. ed. New York: Scribner's, 1961.

Jeremias, Joachim. *The Parables of Jesus*. Rev. ed. New York: Scribner's, 1963.

————. *The Eucharistic Words of Jesus*. Philadelphia: Fortress Press, 1966.

————. *Jerusalem in the Time of Jesus: An Investigation into Economic and Social Conditions During the New Testament Period*. Translated by F. H. and C. H. Cave. Philadelphia: Fortress Press, 1969.

Johnson, Luke Timothy. *The Real Jesus: The Misguided Quest for the Historical Jesus and the Truth of the Traditional Gospels*. Harper San Francisco, 1996.

Josephus, Flavius. *The Jewish War*. Translated by G. A. Williamson. Rev. ed., with new introduction, notes and appendixes by E. Mary Smallwood. Harmondsworth, Middlesex, England; New York: Penguin, 1981, 1970.

Mack, Burton L. *The Lost Gospel: The Book of Q and Christian Origins*. Harper San Francisco, 1993.

McKenzie, John L., S.J. *Dictionary of the Bible*. New York: Macmillan, 1965.

Meeks, Wayne A. *The First Urban Christians: The Social World of the Apostle Paul*. New Haven: Yale University Press, 1983.

Meier, John P. "Jesus." In *New Jerome Biblical Commentary*.

———. *A Marginal Jew: Rethinking the Historical Jesus*. New York: Doubleday, 1991.

Meyer, Marvin, trans. *The Gospel of Thomas: The Hidden Sayings of Jesus*. Interpretation by Harold Bloom. Harper San Francisco, 1992.

The New Jerome Biblical Commentary. Edited by Raymond E. Brown, Joseph A. Fitzmyer, and Roland E. Murphy. Foreword by Carlo Maria Cardinal Martini. Englewood Cliffs, N.J.: Prentice-Hall, 1990.

Perkins, Pheme. "Apocrypha." In *New Jerome Biblical Commentary*.

Perrin, Norman. *Rediscovering the Teaching of Jesus*. New York: Harper & Row, 1976.

Saldarini, Anthony J. "Apocrypha." In *New Jerome Biblical Commentary*.

Sanders, E. P. *The Historical Figure of Jesus*. London: Penguin Press, 1993.

Stark, Rodney. *The Rise of Christianity: A Sociologist Reconsiders History*. Princeton, N.J.: Princeton University Press, 1996.

Suetonius (Gaius Suetonius Tranquillus). *The Twelve Caesars*. Translated by Robert Graves. Revised with introduction by Michael Grant. London; New York; Penguin Books, 1989 [1979].

Tacitus, Cornelius. *The Annals of Imperial Rome*. Translated with an introduction by Michael Grant. Revised with new bibliography. Harmondsworth, England; New York: Penguin Books, 1971.

Vaux, Roland de. *Ancient Israel: Its Life and Institutions*. New York, McGraw-Hill, 1961.

Vermes, Geza. *Jesus the Jew: A Historian's Reading of the Gospels*. Philadelphia: Fortress Press, 1981 [1973].

———. *The Religion of Jesus the Jew*. Minneapolis: Fortress Press, 1993.

Wylen, Stephen M. *The Jews in the Time of Jesus: An Introduction*. Mahwah, N.J.: Paulist Press, 1996.